A Most Gross and Groun

The Denby witchcraft ⟨

To Paul

Every good wish

David Hinchliffe

17/6/2ᴄ.

London League Publications Ltd

A Most Gross and Groundless Prosecution

© David Hinchliffe

The moral right of David Hinchliffe to be identified as the author has been asserted.

Front & back cover design @ Stephen McCarthy.

Front cover photo: Munchcliffe Beck (Photo: David Hinchliffe)

A CIP catalogue record for this book is available from the British Library.

Published in May 2024 by London League Publications Ltd,
PO Box 65784, London NW2 9NS

ISBN: 978-1-909885-37-0

Cover design by Stephen McCarthy Graphic Design
46, Clarence Road, London N15 5BB.

Editing and layout by Peter Lush

Printed and bound in Great Britain by Catford Print Centre, c/o Book Printing Ltd
7 Meridian Centre, Vulcan Way, New Addington, Surrey, CR0 9UG

About the author

David Hinchliffe was MP for Wakefield from 1987 to 2005 and, with the constituency including the Denby area from 1997, he has detailed local knowledge of where the events of 1674 occurred.

David's first book on his sporting passion of Rugby League – *Rugby's Class War* - was published by London League Publications Ltd in 2000 and he has since written and edited a number of other books on the sport.

Along with his wife, Julia, he has a fascination with genealogy and local history. After leaving the Commons, he studied for an MA in Local and Regional History at Leeds University. In 2021, he published his first history book, *Descent into Silence,* about the involvement of his ancestors in a mining tragedy two centuries ago.

David and Julia have two grown-up children and live high in the Pennine hills, not far from Denby.

Thank you

London League Publications Ltd would like to thank Steve McCarthy for designing the cover and the staff of Catford Print Centre for printing the book.

We would also like to thank David and Julia Hinchliffe for the chance to produce this fascinating book.

Dave Farrar and Peter Lush

To see all current books published by London League Publications Ltd, visit www.llpshop.co.uk

Acknowledgements

I have been fortunate to have had the help and encouragement of very many people and organisations while researching and writing this book. I am especially grateful to the following for their support: Richard and Lesley Brook, Maggie Blanshard, David Cook and the High Flatts Friends Meeting, John Hislop, Ruth Sheard, Geoff and Sue Wake, Brian Elliott, Cyril Pearce, David and Jane Raistrick, and Heritage Silkstone, Julie Marshall, the late Prof. Jim Sharpe, Malcolm May, Trevor McDonnell, Chris Heath, Liz Charlesworth, Sarah Greenwood, Bishop Tony Robinson, Rev. Louise Tinniswood, Anthony Bradshaw, Jim Ritchie, Barbara Wilby, Holly Bamford, Marlene Marshall and the Penistone History Archive.

I have particularly appreciated the excellent advice and assistance of staff at Barnsley Archives and Local Studies, Wakefield Libraries and Local Studies, Kirklees Libraries and Local Studies, West Yorkshire Archives, Kirklees, and the West Yorkshire History Centre in Wakefield.

The Denby Dale Parish Council have a longstanding record of encouraging a better understanding of the heritage of their area and I have been grateful for their interest in the book. The advice and support given by Peter Lush and London League Publications has enabled my research on the witchcraft case to be made public.

I owe an enormous debt of gratitude to my wife Julia, for her work in editing the book and her patience with my limited computer skills. Our children, Robert and Rebecca, have also given invaluable support and advice during the book's completion.

Finally, I shall be forever grateful to the late Dr. George Redmonds and the late Prof. David Hey for introducing me, through their remarkable work and personal encouragement, to a passion for genealogy and local history.

Any royalties from this book will be donated to charity.

David Hinchliffe
May 2024

"Our life is love, and peace, and tenderness; and bearing one with another, and forgiving one another, and not laying accusations one against another; but praying one for another, and helping one another up with a tender hand."

Isaac Penington, an early Quaker, in 1667.

Introduction

It was by no means the most notable witchcraft case, but what happened in and around Denby in 1674 would, for those living in the area, have been deeply shocking at the time. During a period of significant religious and political tension, not long after the English Civil Wars and the restoration of the monarchy, a teenage girl came out with a very detailed account of the apparently extensive use of malign powers by a local couple and their married daughter. Her allegations, based largely on claims of overhearing the family's private conversations, had the most serious of implications for those she accused. Detailed testimony was made before local justices, with the case being referred for determination at one of the highest seats of judgment, the county assizes. Remarkably, what was being alleged was very strongly refuted by a large number of local folk, many of whom could be described as of quite high social status. But their formal objections were to be in vain, and perhaps even contributed to the affair coming to a tragic and shocking conclusion.

David Hinchliffe

Fig. 1. The Denby area as depicted in Thomas Jefferys' survey of 1771.
(Courtesy D. Hinchliffe).

Contents

1. A Ready Place

Penning his reflections during the latter half of the 19th century, the Victorian historian, William Wheater, of Headingley, Leeds, waxed lyrical of the time a black gloom had enveloped his County of Yorkshire, covering the entire land. "That black gloom was of witch influence, horrible, portentous, monstrous, fiendish. The witches were abroad...", he wrote, "...restless and uncontrolled in their action and malignity; demons, to encounter whom was sometimes death, always loss and misery."[1]

By the time he was writing of "Witches and Wizards," in a chapter on "Yorkshire Superstitions," Wheater was able to pour scorn on the historic cruelties of Government-appointed 'witchfinders', like the notorious Matthew Hopkins,[2] but implied that past witch-hunts had merely shifted occultism's locus. "It was compelled to desert the castle and the baronial hall, but it found good shelter beneath the thatched roof of the rustic or beside the loom of the weaver, and there it tarried,[3]" he suggested. In other words, the organised pursuit of witchcraft had, in Wheater's opinion, merely driven it 'down market'.

Strikingly, he went further, suggesting that Yorkshire, in particular, was peculiarly receptive to such practices. "Nature gave the county high rugged hills, wild trackless moors, bogs, moist and gloom; and so fitted it to become one of the last earthly resting-places of glamour,"[4] he asserted, with the natives particularly susceptible. "The minds of Yorkshiremen are naturally somewhat prone to melancholy and given to wonder. The weird and mysterious have ever found in them a ready place,"[5] he added.

In terms of topography, Wheater couldn't have offered a clearer description of exactly what the small Pennine settlement of Denby, near Huddersfield, would have looked like during 1674, when disturbing suggestions of sorcery in the area came to light. A married couple, Joseph and Susanna Hinchliffe, and their married daughter, Anne Shillitoe, had suddenly found themselves at the centre of claims that they possessed, and had in fact used, evil powers, to the serious detriment of others.

Perhaps one of the more striking aspects of the Denby accusations is that they were made when what had been widely regarded as a witchcraft 'craze' within Britain and Western Europe was in marked and obvious decline. One account of this country's experience attributes decreasing allegations to scientific advances and a growing knowledge of anatomy and physiology by the latter half of the C17th. "The realm of magic, of witches and spells, was abandoned by the educated. Within a generation of 1640 the prosecution of witches had almost ceased."[6] They had risen here from the mid-C16th, reaching their highest level during its final two decades. By 1674, accusations involving alleged witchcraft were diminishing significantly and the last known British execution, following a 'proven' case, was just eight years later, at Exeter in 1682.

As we approach almost three and a half centuries since they occurred, a detailed look at the events of 1674 - which at the time shocked the West Riding community affected – is long overdue. The allegations made about malefic acts and the possession of evil powers have received some passing attention from local historians over the years. But no description of what went on at the time has set out with the specific aim of trying to better understand the full detail of who was involved, their backgrounds, and, as far as can be determined, what exactly occurred. Within the constraints of the limited local archive evidence and primary sources of material from the C17th, I hope this account might add a little more to the insights which already exist into an affair which has never been completely forgotten but never fully understood.

It is important to be clear from the outset that, although this book is based upon claims concerning supposed witchcraft, it is not intended to be primarily about witchcraft. That subject has received enormous attention over very many years from historians, anthropologists, psychologists, and feminists, as well as non-academic novelists and storytellers who have fictionalised tales from past reported episodes. Most – if not all of them – will have known far more about the subject than me. One authority suggests that "…it is difficult to think of any other historical problem over which there is more disagreement and confusion."[7] It is not my intention to add to it.

My purpose is not to enlarge upon the very weighty assortment of literature in an already well-explored field of enquiry. Rather, it is to use what appears to be an allegation of witchcraft to try to understand a little more about life and relationships within a West Riding Pennine parish in the second half of the C17th, a historically turbulent period. The case in question clearly raised considerable public concern among some - but by no means all - in the locality, occurring at a time in our history when religious and political tensions were rife. Parliament's requirement in 1642 for all adult males in England and Wales to swear an oath to the Protestant faith had been designed to isolate Roman Catholicism, the revival of which was feared under Charles I. The English Civil Wars of 1642-6 had divided families and communities. The execution of Charles in 1649 had been followed by the rule of the Commonwealth Government and the rapidity of the collapse of this 'republic' has, for many, always been difficult to fully comprehend. It is, perhaps, best explained by the suggestion that its ending simply reflected "…the fragility of its creation."[8] Downing and Millman's study of the Civil Wars offered that proposition and concluded that the Commonwealth "… could never resolve the many contradictions underlying its existence. There was a widespread desire for a civilian form of government that could never be reconciled with the fact that from December 1648 authority ultimately came from the Army." [9]

While there is clearly merit in considering this bigger constitutional picture, others would suggest that the Commonwealth failed to survive for the simple reason that its rigidly puritanical ideology denied ordinary folk even the most limited opportunities for escapism and enjoyment in their pursuit of what was deemed a 'godly' life. When maypole dancing to celebrate May Day and even

Christmas festivities were frowned upon, as the Spen Valley historian, Frank Peel, put it "...they rebelled against the edicts of the sour-faced ascetics..."[10] For him, the basic explanation for the demise of the republic was its active suppression of the very limited joys in life at the time. "Of all the mistakes made by the noble-minded men who struck so manfully in defence of English liberty when it was in sore peril, this was the greatest and helped forward the Restoration of King Charles (the Second) more doubtless than any other."[11]

The restoration of the monarchy and the crowning of Charles II in 1660 did not deliver the greater religious toleration which many had hoped for. A series of Acts of Uniformity were passed, with one, enforced from 1662, requiring clergy of the Church of England to conform to a revised Book of Common Prayer. It has been argued that "The upper classes wanted to close the door for good on the religious radicalism and experimentation of the Commonwealth and return to an older, more stable form of worship."[12] But, instead, it led directly to the growth of Protestant non-conformity, the influence of which became increasingly apparent within the south Yorkshire parish of Penistone. That parish contained what was then known as the township of Denby, where it was alleged, evil deeds were to take place just a dozen years later.

2. Malefic allegations

It is difficult not to gain the impression that these allegations of witchcraft, made against three local folk from the same family, were a cause of significant concern well beyond the scattered cottages in the upland areas of Upper and Lower Denby. Quite remarkably, what was being claimed about them generated considerable disquiet in the local community. Some of the most wealthy and influential people in their immediate neighbourhood and further afield were to become involved with the case and, in many instances, make known their deep unease at the accusations being made.

What would then just have been the tiny, separated hamlets and farmsteads making up the then 'Over' and 'Nether' Denby, were, during the C17th, part of the sizeable parish of Penistone which stretched, at that time, from the Cheshire border in the west almost to Silkstone in the east, and from near Midhope, close to the Derbyshire border in the south, almost to Emley, to the east of Huddersfield, in the north. The Parish Church of St John the Baptist stands high up in Penistone itself. We are told that "In days gone by the curfew bell would be rung at sunset, and on foggy nights a bell would be used to guide travellers who might be lost on the moors near the town."[13] Covering not far off 23,000 acres - and much of it moorland – the parish was divided for administrative purposes into eight townships, of which Denby was one.

In terms of understanding the make-up of Upper and Lower Denby and the wider Penistone parish at this time, it is fortunate that the Hearth Tax assessment undertaken at the then official start of 1672 gives a quite detailed account of local householders. Lady Day, on 25 March, was an important date in the calendar then. Along with Michaelmas, on 29 September, it was the date twice-yearly rents were paid. But, until 1752, Lady Day had also marked the New Year, so this account of 17th century events uses the standard 1674/5 format for dates from 1 January to 25 March.

Fig. 2. The Parish Church of St. John, the Baptist, Penistone.
(Dransfield, 1906).

The published returns from the assessment of tax liability, based upon the number of hearths within a property, enable some idea to be gained of the total of people then resident in a particular area. From the 53 properties recorded in the township of Denby,[14] using a suggested multiplier of 4.5 occupants in each house,[15] a total population of just short of 240, in and near the two hamlets, seems likely at the time. It is not unreasonable to assume that local residents would be fairly well acquainted with each other, as they would no doubt be with others from nearby villages, hamlets and farmsteads. What can only be viewed as a very rough idea of the comparative wealth of these local households is possible through the individual hearth numbers declared. The impression is gained from a brief perusal of the returns that, with 18 of the properties declaring 3 or more hearths, Denby was far from being an impoverished community. Indeed, only one householder among the 53 – a William Hamshire[16] – was exempted from liability, either as a consequence of being in receipt of poor relief from the parish or paying less than £1 in annual rent.

While the witch 'craze' may well have been on the wane by the time of the Denby case, its 'presence' within the lives of vast numbers during the Elizabethan and Stuart periods should not be underestimated. One study of the phenomenon suggested "All classes were concerned from Pope to peasant, from Queen to cottage gill."[17] During a time long before the advent of broadcast and social media, apart from the church pulpit, daily gossip would be the main news channel in rural communities. As James Sharpe has suggested, "In such an environment there is little doubt that witchcraft suspicions were among the more avidly discussed of topics."[18]

The two households which were implicated in the 1674 allegations would appear, at the time of the assessment two years earlier, to have been living in either adjacent or nearby properties as they are listed next to each other in the return. The respective male family heads are recorded as Joseph Hinchliffe and Thomas Shillitoe, both of whom are noted as having just one hearth.[19] The returns do not include information on householders' occupations, but, as John Morrill has noted, "...'industry' in the seventeenth century took place in cottages and outbuildings of rural village communities" with textiles "by far the largest 'manufacture'..." particularly in the Pennine region.[20] It is probably not unreasonable to conclude that data contained in the first national census, nearly 140 years later - albeit with a local population probably four times larger - gives a rough breakdown of the main economic activity. The Denby of 1801 was overwhelmingly populated by weavers.[21]

It is difficult to appreciate now the extent to which extensive religious persecution was a central feature of life in parishes such as Penistone during the 17th century, particularly around the time of the Denby case. Fletcher's portrayal of "Yorkshiremen of the Restoration" focuses particularly on the period from 1642 to 1680 and vividly brings to life what was happening: "The Puritans turned out the Anglican clergy to beg their bread; Anglicanism, under the aegis of the State, ejected clergy inclined to Presbyterianism; Puritans and Anglicans coalesced in hunting down Roman Catholics, and in making the life of the Quaker almost unbearable."[22]

There had been very real fears during the reign of Charles I of a gradual return to Catholicism and it was the Puritans who increasingly appeared as the main opposition to both an autocratic monarchy and the influence of Catholic theology within the Church of England. These tensions played out in very many communities at the time and the importance of the appointment of an incumbent sympathetic to local thinking is very apparent from what went on in Penistone. John Hewitt's 1863 history of Wakefield outlined the way in which, as far back as 1597, the presentation to the living of Penistone had been agreed as a shared right, so that in 1602, it was in the hands of Godfrey Copley, Esq; in 1619, in the gift of John Savile, Esq.; in 1633 and 1635, George Burdett had it in his gift; then by 1642 Sir William Saville had assumed the right to present. A regular visitor to Penistone parish in 1674 was the travelling Presbyterian minister, Oliver Heywood and he succinctly summed up some of the local tensions. "This was in the troublesome time of the interregnum; and the parishioners at one time annually elected a vicar themselves. The vicar, or rather minister, as he, being a parliamentarian, would call himself, was in possession of this living when the Act of Uniformity was passed, at the restoration. His name was Henry Swift. He was, on several occasions, committed to Wakefield Prison for not complying with the Act. In spite of this he continued to preach in this church up to 1689, when he died."[23]

Any examination of life in the Penistone parish during the second half of the 17th century cannot fail to draw the conclusion that Swift's survival during the religious repressions from 1662 until his death was very much a consequence of prominent local families in the area, who had traditionally 'presented' the living, being actively concerned to preserve dissent. Not only did several of them strongly support his ministry but they also clearly encouraged other prominent dissenters to preach during this time at St John the Baptist. Oliver Heywood was undoubtedly a frequent visitor to the Church, accommodated by these families, and it is his brief note of affairs in Denby in 1674 which was to prove a rather important record.

Fig 3. The Rev. Oliver Heywood (Peel, 1891)

One account of what are described as the "Denbigh" (sic) allegations rather downplays the story of Heywood's life as an "obscure source" of information regarding what exactly happened.[24] But it is largely thanks to Heywood's personally recorded visitations within the wider Penistone parish that we are aware of the local developments of 1674 and the public reaction to what became widely known allegations of evil-doing made in the locality. The depictions of Heywood create an interesting image. In noting his frequent presence a few miles to the north west over in the Spen Valley, Frank

9

Peel wrote of "This wonderfully active evangelist."[25] J. S. Fletcher notably terms Heywood as "...this sturdy old itinerant of the sombre border-country of Yorkshire and Lancashire (representing) the gulf which lay between those who stopped in and those who went out of the Church of England in the early days of the Restoration."[26] Heywood had, according to Fletcher "...a pretty trick of putting down in his journal a great many matters of interest to humanity."[27] A good example of this is Heywood's brief "Event Book" reference to "One Joseph Hinchlive (sic) and his wife being accused of witchcraft".[28] It contains just a short paragraph summarising an affair which – nearly three and a half centuries on – is long overdue for a more detailed examination.

3. All the attributes of a Witch

It was, first and foremost, a longstanding interest in genealogy which drew me to allegations being made against some individuals who, according to the 1672 Hearth Tax returns for Denby,[29] share my surname, or a variant of it. My own paternal Hinchliffe ancestors seem to have been connected to nearby Cumberworth, just a couple of miles to the north west, with my Great-Great grandfather, Jehoshaphat Hinchliffe, being baptised at St. Nicholas Church there in 1791. The earliest Hinchliffe entry in the Cumberworth registers appears to be a baptism in 1764 – less than a century on from the witchcraft case - but this certainly does not mark the surname's arrival here. Its origins stem from a long abandoned medieval settlement in the hills to the north west of Holmfirth but its first known recorded occurrence outside the Holme Valley seems to be evidenced in the 1379 Poll Tax payment of four pence by Adam de Hyncheclyf and Elizabet (sic), his daughter, actually in Cumberworth.[30] What I once thought was a rather unusual surname is, with its numerous variants, in actual fact quite common in the old West Riding of Yorkshire, with at least fifty separate households noted back then, amongst a far smaller population in 1672 than we have today.[31]

But, while Penistone parish featured at the time several families from this total, the township of Denby featured just one, 'headed' – as the Hearth Tax returns noted – by Joseph Hinchliffe. There are few clues as to his origins but, if Joseph was a family name, there was another Joseph Hinchliffe elsewhere in the Penistone parish – in Langsett – just a couple of years before the witchcraft allegations were made.[32] However, there do appear to be indications that Joseph's origins may have been from beyond the Penistone parish boundaries. On 30 April, 1639, the Wakefield parish registers record the marriage of a Joseph Hinchliffe to a Susan Clayton. Neither surname appears common in Wakefield during the C17th, with no Hinchliffes and just one Clayton household recorded there in 1672.[33]

Hinchliffes were, however, resident in the village of Woolley, between Wakefield and Barnsley and some five miles to the north-east of Denby, from at least as far back as the first half of the C15th.[34] But while three or four separate families of that name are recorded there earlier in the C17th, by the time of the Denby case the surname's presence was minimal. What appears to have been something of a population crisis in the post-restoration period clearly impacted quite significantly in the locality. One analysis of the chapelry of Woolley and its mother parish of Royston shows that, during the eight years from the winter of 1665/6 to the autumn of 1673, burials were two to eight times above the norm.[35] The burial of a "Thomas Hinsliffe", the son of John, is recorded at Woolley on 30 April, 1661, but by the 1672 Hearth Tax, the sole resident there with the surname is "Widdow Hinchcliffe."[36] The burial of "An Hinchlive widdowe" at Woolley Church, on 2 August, 1673, would seem to not just mark her passing but also the disappearance of the surname from the village for several decades. The Clayton surname, however, features more widely around this time. While the Wakefield marriage might confirm to the norm at the time for marriages to take place within the bride's home parish, the Hearth Tax returns do note Claytons also resident in Denby, High Hoyland, Clayton West and Emley by then.[37]

In trying to establish some identity for Joseph, it has been suggested that his occupation was that of a labourer[38] although the sources of this information are not clear. There may be a little more evidence to support Chris Heath's view, concerning the 1674 case, that "The drama could have initially been played out in Lower Denby..."[39], or Nether Denby as it was then known, as some of the key witnesses in the case appear to be from, or living close to, that location. And the likelihood is that the Hinchliffes were, indeed, of quite humble stock. The Hearth Tax returns record that they were among less than half of all Denby's households at the time having just the basics, possessing only one hearth.

Less than 20 years earlier, not far away at Newton, just to the north of Wakefield, Jennet Benton (or Benson) had been committed to York Assizes, accused of witchcraft. One detailed account of her case suggests she "... had a fierce black cat that hissed and spat at anyone who approached",[40]reinforcing the idea she kept a 'familiar', a spirit or demon supposedly in the service of the Devil. A rather more imaginative telling of Benton's case claimed that, as well as the black cat, she had what were regarded as all the attributes of a witch, being "A stooped-backed, wizened old crone with a baleful eye..."[41] We have no means of knowing what Joseph Hinchliffe's wife, Susanna, looked like in 1674 but, with her being an older woman and, perhaps, in her mid-fifties by then, if the 1639 wedding record is to be believed, it is worth noting that such perceptions were clearly quite widespread around the time. The Barnsley historian, Eli Hoyle's, early 20th century writing reminds us that, in those days, witchcraft was thoroughly believed in. "And heavy and severe were the punishments meted out to those poor persons – chiefly old women – who became the objects of suspicion."[42]

Beyond the Hearth Tax detail, the parish registers from the period offer little help in establishing a detailed picture of Susanna and her background but we know that Anne, her daughter and fellow accused, was, by 1672, married to Thomas Shillitoe. The parish records for Royston, also between Wakefield and Barnsley, began in 1557 and evidence what appears to be their marriage on 24 February, 1662/3. The then Anne Hinchliffe is described as being of the parish of Penistone and William Paver's Marriage Licenses give her age as 19 at the time. Thomas's age is given as 23, he is described as a 'yeoman' and this source, while having the same date for the marriage, notes the location of the wedding as Penistone.[43] A possible explanation might be banns having been read in both parishes, with this being what was recorded.

Paver, a Yorkshire genealogist, produced extracts of original documents from the York Registry during the 19th century and these have been published by the Yorkshire Archaeological Society. While the YAS is likely to have scrupulously reproduced Paver's records, his account of the venue is clearly contradicted by the entry in the Royston register and his according the groom the status of 'yeoman' could also be questionable, bearing in mind the Shillitoes were living in an apparently quite humble abode in Denby nearly a decade later. The 'yeoman' label had described, from Tudor times, the social class below gentry: the better-off farmers working what was usually, but not always, their own land. But, as Hey has made clear, the personal wealth needed to attain this status varied considerably from area to area and over time.[44]

The longstanding line of Hinchliffes residing in Woolley may have ended in 1673 but the Royston marriage record of Thomas Shillitoe and Anne Hinchliffe could offer an important clue regarding her paternal family origins. The village of Woolley was, at this time, within the Royston parish, so Anne could well have been marrying within the parish of her birth. The likelihood, therefore, is that Joseph Hinchliffe of Denby was descended from a branch of the Hinchliffe family with longstanding connections to Woolley going back to at least 1430, when a William Hynchclyff was bequeathed 20s. in the will of Oliver Woderow.[45] The Woderow or Woodrove family held the Woolley estate until it passed to a branch of the Wentworth family in 1599. I am sure it had no bearing whatsoever on Woolley's later role in the determination of the 1674 case but the Woolley Hinchliffes do appear to have had a rather questionable reputation. Commenting on the minutes of the twice-yearly tourns held at Barnsley during the reign of Henry V1, Barnsley historian, Rowland Jackson, wrote "These Woolley people appear to have been desperate rogues, especially William Hinchliffe."[46] To be fair to him, alleged offences concerning the likes of brewing ales and taking excess profits, playing forbidden games and failing to repair hedges, dating from 1433 to 1510, will clearly have involved more than one William Hinchliffe.

While questioning Paver's summary of Thomas and Anne's marriage record, the likelihood of the groom being in his early twenties at the time is quite probable. Some ten miles to the north east of Denby lies the parish of Warmfield, between Wakefield and Normanton, consisting of the villages of Heath, Kirkthorpe and Warmfield itself. This parish stands out in Phillimore's Atlas and Index of Parish Registers as a "Peculiar",[47] having an exemption from the jurisdiction of the local church authorities which can complicate some historic research. Nevertheless, the Warmfield parish records denote the baptism at Kirkthorpe Church of a "Thomas Shillito" on 20 February, 1638/9. While the Protestation Returns of 1641/2 record an adult by the name of "Thomas Shilletoe" in "Warmfield:Kirkthorpe", the baptismal entry appears to be the only other mention of a person of this name in what might be termed the locality around the time we can assume he was born. The later Hearth Tax noted that, of just over fifty households recorded in the Warmfield parish during 1672, five had the Shillitoe surname.

Fig 4. Church of St. Peter, the Apostle, Kirkthorpe, in the parish of Warmfield-cum-Heath. (D. Hinchliffe).

Thomas's father is recorded as "Francis" and a Francis Shillitoe is among those noted in the Hearth Tax, occupying a three-hearth property in the area. The identification of a person of this name leads on to other interesting questions about the reasons for a possible connection between Warmfield and close to Denby, the location of the witchcraft allegation. "Francis Shillitoe of Warmfield" was bequeathed some land in Cawthorne on 31 January, 1654/5, under the will of a William Oley, of Heath.[48] The Oleys seem to have quite a significant presence in the Wakefield area and in Warmfield parish, owning Eshald House in Heath, the site of the more modern Heath Hall, from the 1640s, according to one source.[49] During that same decade, the Parliamentarian captain, Adam Eyre, of Hazlehead, near Penistone, recorded his visits to Wakefield to a cloth merchant named "Danyell Oley"[50] and the later reference to a "Mr Daniell Olley" of Wakefield in the Hearth Tax returns[51] suggests a local family of some substance.

According to the Commonwealth Probate Index, Francis Shillitoe seems to have undertaken the role of 'executor' following William's death, with the will being proven on 15 November, 1654.[52] He is identified in it as "Yeoman" and the property involved is described as "Rowleys in Cawthorne Lanes".[53] Subsequent transactions, some two decades later, indicate that a "Joseph Oley of the Heath, Par. Warmfield, Yeoman" had land in Cawthorne tenanted by a Joseph Butterworth during September, 1674[54] and five closes there were sold by this particular Oley the following month.[55] From the articles of agreement concerning this sale, it is made clear that the land termed "Rowleys" was located at Jowett House, just to the south west of Cannon Hall. While this term could have originally come from a connection to a local family of that name, or, indeed, its association with the Oleys, it is much more likely to have arisen from an original reference to it being the local term for a rough clearing. One account of a survey of lands in Cawthorne, taken in January, 1648, makes clear that land clearance had quite recently taken place in that immediate locality. D. J. Smith writes that "...4 acres of former woodland at

Jowett House was noted as 'now made arable', 5 acres of springwood at the same place under another tenancy had also been cleared."[56] The tree covering from what is known as Deffer Wood is likely to have stretched further to the south in the C17th and probably been closer to Jowett House than is now the case. It does therefore seem that the Shillitoes could have held – and, possibly for a short time, worked - land less than two miles from Lower Denby and Paver's 'yeoman' categorisation of Thomas Shillitoe would make a little more sense if this was the case.

The suggestion that Shillitoe, his wife and her parents, were likely to have lived at or near Lower Denby by the time of the 1674 case, has more credibility if one or more of them may at some point have been working this land close to Jowett House. As the earliest census returns for the Denby area, albeit many years later, note the only Shillitoes remaining in the township as being resident at Upper Bagden,[57] between Denby and High Hoyland, were Shillitoe, his wife and her parents, residing further to the east of Denby than has previously been thought? While Upper Bagden, on Pool Hill Lane, Denby, is now the site of a small estate of several sizeable modern houses, a farmstead existed there from "the middle decades of the 17th Century," according to a Historic Environment Record held by West Yorkshire Archives Service.[58] The likelihood is that it could well have been occupied during the 16th Century as a marriage settlement concerning a "John Haigh of Over Bagden, Denby, Yorks., yeoman…" is dated as far back as 1604.[59]

In the bequest to Francis Shillitoe of January, 1654/5, William Oley is described as 'Clerk', with the implication that he had a formal role within the Church and it appears that there may well have been some ongoing devotional commitment within that family as a Francis Oley is noted by the Penistone historian, John Dransfield, to have been Vicar of Penistone between 1602 and 1619.[60] The fact that probably the same person, being described as a 'Clerk', features in a Cawthorne tithing document in 1623,[61] also indicates the family's presence to the south of the old West Riding.

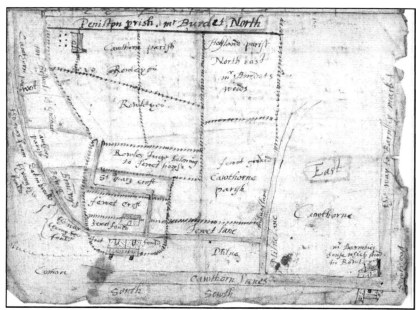

Fig. 5. This map is included in papers from c.1628 concerning a case relating to a right of way through Jowett House fold to Rowleys, near Cawthorne. Sp. St. 143/1-4. Jowett House is located just over half a mile to the south west of Cannon Hall and Rowleys can be seen marked on the map to the north of the House. (Reproduced by kind permission of Barnsley Archives and Local Studies)

Francis Oley would appear to have had acquired the Cawthorne land from the Hawksworth family of Denby some ten years earlier. There is documentary evidence from 1613 that the widowed Helen Hawksworth of Upper Denby had, on 7 June that year, passed to her son, John, of Lower Denby, "...all her right and title in the toft or tenement called Rowley alias Holdrughley, in Cawthorne..." which he had been working at the time. Three weeks later, on 22 June, 1613, John Hawksworth sold the land to Francis Oley [62] and it would therefore seem that it was being cultivated some years before the clearance mentioned in the 1648 land survey.

A plaque on the south wall of St Peter's Church, Kirkthorpe, offers some clarification of the Oleys' connection with Warmfield-cum-

Heath, listing the incumbents there over several centuries. A Francis Oley is recorded as vicar from 1619 until his death in 1643, when he was succeeded by his eldest son, William, who served from 1643 until his death during March, 1653. The Protestation Returns for Warmfield:Kirkthorpe, collected shortly before Francis Oley passed away, indicate that "Francis Shelitoe" was an official involved in their completion in his role as churchwarden at the time. Bearing in mind the adversity which was to later engulf Shillitoe's son, Thomas, it is an interesting coincidence that widely reported allegations of witchcraft were made in the parish during 1650, while they were resident there. Both the Shillitoes and the Oley brothers would undoubtedly have known Margaret Morton of Kirkthorpe and her accuser, Joan Booth of Warmfield.

It seems that Francis Shillitoe's holding of the Cawthorne land was at least in part for the purpose of settling William Oley's tithing liabilities and the payment of some legacies which probably required the land to be worked directly by its owner or by a tenant. But, at the time of its subsequent acquisition by Heath's Joseph Oley, in the same year as the Denby case, it was in the hands of the late William Oley's younger brother, Barnabas. He had been born in 1602 and, like his father and older brother, also entered the church. William had studied at Clare College, Cambridge, and, after similarly studying there and becoming a Fellow in 1623, Barnabas became vicar of St Bartholomew's Church, in Great Gransden, Cambridgeshire in 1633.

The period of ownership of this land by Barnabas Oley may have been complicated by the fact that he was an active supporter of Charles 1 during the period of the English Civil wars. He had been involved in raising funds from his old university for Charles and ejection from his parish, as well as fines, followed in 1644. During subsequent years, until the restoration of the monarchy, he moved around the country, spending some of the time back in his brother's West Riding parish. The possibility that a formal relationship existed between Francis Shillitoe and Barnabas Oley is suggested by a document within the Spencer-Stanhope archives describing Shillitoe, at the end of January,

1654/5, as "Yeoman to" Oley who is at this time described as "… of Heath, Par. Of Warmfield, Clerk."[63] Following the restoration of the monarchy, Barnabas Oley returned as incumbent at Great Gransden in 1660. It is not clear precisely when he acquired the ownership of the Cawthorne fields but, in view of his strong Royalist sympathies, and consequent vulnerability during the Commonwealth period, it may have been to his personal benefit that this land was held for a time, and possibly worked, by the Shillitoes.

Without the availability of a definite baptismal record, recorded ages at the time of marriage or death are often unreliable until very recent times but it is not unlikely, during the latter half of the C17th, that Anne Shillitoe would have been marrying around the age of 19 or 20. This would suggest that Susanna, her mother, was probably well into middle age and, perhaps, late middle age at the time the allegations were made, with Anne unlikely to have been her first daughter. The Penistone parish registers do contain a record of the baptism of a "Josephus Hinchcliffe" on 3 November, 1661, whose father is recorded as "Josephi", but, it is unlikely, although not impossible, this would relate to the Denby family, as others with the surname are recorded as living in both Langsett and Thurlstone, within the parish, around this time.[64] It is known that, by the 1650s, Joseph was the tenth most commonly used male first name in England and also that, by then, the earlier practice of naming a child after a god-parent had been replaced by the more frequent use of parental names.[65] But we do not know if Susanna's husband was residing in Denby, or even the Penistone parish, in 1661 and the register entry does not name a paternal residence or the name of the child's mother. If the entry was for Susanna and Joseph's son, the possibility is that he may have been one of their first children – perhaps their first boy – bearing in mind his being given his father's name. As Anne would have been born around 1644, it is doubtful that it would have taken until 1661 to conceive their first son. The naming of a child after an earlier deceased one of the same name was not unknown at the time but we are, perhaps, clutching at straws here.

From where Joseph and Susanna Hinchliffe originated is difficult to establish with certainty. My own research into the ramification of their surname and its variants within the old West Riding, from its first use within the Graveship of Holme within the C14th through to the 1672 Hearth Tax, concluded that, by the C17th, while the name remained most commonly used within its area of origin, near to Holmfirth, specific clusters could be noted in the Leeds area, the village of Woolley, near Wakefield, and the parish of Penistone. As has been noted, the Denby of 1674 was within that parish and its boundaries, at the time of the witchcraft case, included Cumberworth, with the longstanding Hinchliffe connections also previously mentioned. But, of course, both Cumberworth and Denby are close to the Kirkburton Parish whose registers record more Hinchliffe entries than anywhere else.

Susan, and its variants, was among the 10 most popular girls' names by the end of the 17th century[66] and the practice of naming offspring after parents is likely to have been similar with girls during the period immediately before the witchcraft allegations. The only Penistone baptismal entry for a Susanna Hinchliffe around this time is dated 30 October, 1666, with – again – no mother noted and the father given as Johannis Hinchliffe. Recording errors did occur quite frequently when illiterate folk gave their names for formal recording by people unfamiliar with local accents but, once more, it is speculation to connect this Susanna with the Denby family.

4. Parties to the particular

The Denby case involved four distinct parties. As well as the Hinchliffes and their daughter, Anne Shillitoe, there was the accuser, Mary Moor, the Haighs, who were alleged to be the subjects of certain malefic acts and an Elizabeth Brooke, of Clayton, who testified to witnessing the apparent impact of malefic acts upon Moor.

Moor was a 16-year-old girl who lived in nearby Clayton, nowadays more often known as Clayton West. The location of Clayton Hall probably indicates the reason for the more recent addition of 'West', as the bulk of the village's development in recent times has been between what is now Clayton Hall Farm, just to the north of the former High Hoyland Church, Bilham Grange, to the farm's south west, and Scissett and Skelmanthorpe to its west. As John Wilkinson pointed out in his study of the upper Dearne valley, "What was once a small agricultural settlement within the parish of High Hoyland was to be transformed by the Industrial Revolution."[67] In the same way as the scattered communities around what was known as Denby Dike, in the Dearne valley to the north of Denby, became the sizeable village of Denby Dale through industrialisation, Clayton's focus was shifted firmly towards the higher Pennine hills to the west.

The 1672 Hearth Tax return for what is then just termed 'Clayton' features less than forty separate households. Amongst them is that 'headed' by a "John Moore", with a two-hearth liability, and the likelihood is that he was Mary's father as a John Moor featured in her deposition, having allegedly suffered from what were claimed to be malefic acts. There is little to inform us of John Moor's background, but it has been noted that an inscription in the tower of High Hoyland Church, dated 1679, records a mason of this name having been involved the Church's reconstruction around this time.[68] High Hoyland was within easy walking distance of Clayton.

How Mary Moor knew mother and daughter, Hinchliffe and Shillitoe is not immediately apparent but, back in the 17th century, there would have been considerable movement between the various local villages and hamlets in the area, particularly by those working as farm labourers in seasonal employment or, all year round, in service with local gentry. While women undoubtedly would have helped out in the fields at times of particular demand with, for example, harvesting, if they were not directly concerned with weaving or child-care within the home, their involvement in domestic service in their immediate locality or further afield was quite common. This was a particular option for girls as they were growing up and the diaries of the Parliamentary captain, Adam Eyre of Hazlehead, make clear that the practice of taking on neighbours' daughters for such work was common in the Penistone parish during the mid-17th century.[69]

In trying to understand Mary Moor's contact with Denby at this time, some appreciation of the highways, tracks and pathways existing during the latter half of the C17th is helpful. In particular, it is especially important to recognise the tendency then to use higher level routes, which drained better in wet weather, and long predated the likes of today's A636 Wakefield-Denby Dale Road, the A635 Barnsley-Shepley Lane Road and the A629 Ingbirchworth-Shepley Lane Head Road. If Moor worked in the wider Denby area – as seems quite likely – her route to and from there would probably take her

past Toppitt Farm by Deffer Hill, on Bagden Lane to Upper Bagden and either along Brow Lane, south towards Denby Hall, or Pool Hill Lane to Dry Hill and Lower Denby. Of course, it is conceivable that Susanna Hinchliffe, Anne Shillitoe, or both of them, knew Moor through travelling in the opposite direction for work but, as will be noted, the evidence she presented suggests not.

Left: Fig. 6. Brow Lane (D. Hinchliffe)

23

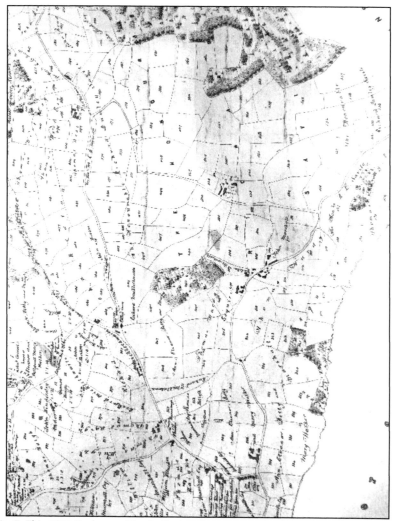

Fig. 7. This 1802 Enclosure Map indicates the routes around Lower Denby some 130 years on from the 'witchcraft' case. The cottages of Lower Denby Lane are marked, with Papist Hall just to the east along Denby Lane. The track from Denby Hall along Brow Lane can be seen, joining Pool Hill Lane at Upper Bagden. Deffer Wood is marked to the east of the map.
(West Yorkshire Archives, Kirklees. WYK 1978/2/DD1802)

Moor gave very detailed accounts of what she claimed to have witnessed, mainly in relation to evil acts she overheard being discussed by Hinchliffe and Shillitoe. We are fortunate that the depositions presented to the justices at the time are held in the National Archives and, although very difficult to read, do give a good deal of detail of what was then being alleged. So much of her account relates to detailed conversations taking place between the two accused, which Moor claimed to have overheard. Her statements offer a comprehensive history of the apparent dialogue between mother and daughter and attained, perhaps, more credibility by relating questions asked where Moor discloses she was unable to hear the answer given.

The central testimony was the one sworn by Moor on 26 August, 1674, which claimed that: *on 14th day of August, shee heard Susann, wife of Joseph Hinchliffe, and Ann, wife of Thomas Shillitoe, of Denby, discoursing thus together. The said Susann said to Ann, if thou canst but get young Thomas Haigh to buy thee three pennyworth of indicoe, and look him in the face when he gives it to thee, and touch his locks, we shall have power enough to take life. And shee also said, Nanny wilt thou not go today and make hay at Thomas Haigh's? To which the same Ann answered, Yes. Then said the said Susan, if that canst but bring nyne bitts of bread away, and nyne bitts of butter in thy mouth, wee shall have power enough to take the life of their goods. They need not be in such pomp, for wee will nether leave them cowe nor horse at house. The said Ann asked the said Susan, Mother did you doe Dame Haigh any hurt? The said Susan answered That did I, for after I toucht the cadgeings of her skirts, shee stept not many steps after. I shortened her walk. And this informant says that at another time before, she heard the said Susan say to the said Ann, I think I must give this Thomas Bramhall over, for they tye so much whigen about him, I cannot come to my purpose, else I could have worn him away once in two yeares. Then said the said Ann to the said Susan her mother, would I was as free as I was within this two years. The said Susan replied thou art too farr worne. Then the said Susan said to her daughter, Nanny did thou not hear that Timothy Haigh had like to have been drowned in the Quaker Hall dyke? To which shee answered shee did not hear. Then the said Susan said, I lead him up and down the Moor with an intention hee should either have broak his neck or have drownd himself; but at last his horse threw him, and hee then went over the bridge, and I had a foot in. How hee gott over the bridge I cannot tell, except the Lord lead him by the hand. And then shee sayd, I had him not at the time; but the next time, lett the horse and him look both to themselves. The said Ann askt the said Susan, her mother, if ever shee had done John Moor any hurt? To which shee answered yes, and sayd, I took the life of two swine and did hurt to a childe. And this informant further saith, that shee heard the said Susan say to the said Ann, that if her father had but toucht Martha Haigh,, before shee had spoken to him, they could have had power enough to have taken away her life. To which the said Ann replied, there is noe time byepast.*

Just below the detailed account of Moor's allegations there is a short note in Latin confirming that the deposition had been sworn that day at Woolley before a magistrate named Wentworth. In what appears to be the same hand as that of his signature, at the bottom of the document are the words "to be bound over to Assizes."

It is something of a challenge to come to an understanding of what was actually being alleged in her statement but, in view of his disposal of the case, the magistrate clearly took it very seriously. A number of third parties feature in Moor's evidence and the Haigh family are given particular prominence. Moor mentions Susanna Hinchliffe speaking to Shillitoe about gaining power over "young Thomas Haigh" after he had bought "three pennyworth of indicoe". We know that the Denby area was traditionally well populated by weavers so it is likely that both of the accused and Moor would be familiar with the use of indigo, a permanent dye, originally obtained from the leaves of woad. These had at first been imported from France in the C16th until the religious wars of the time led to the plant being grown on an increasingly large scale in England.

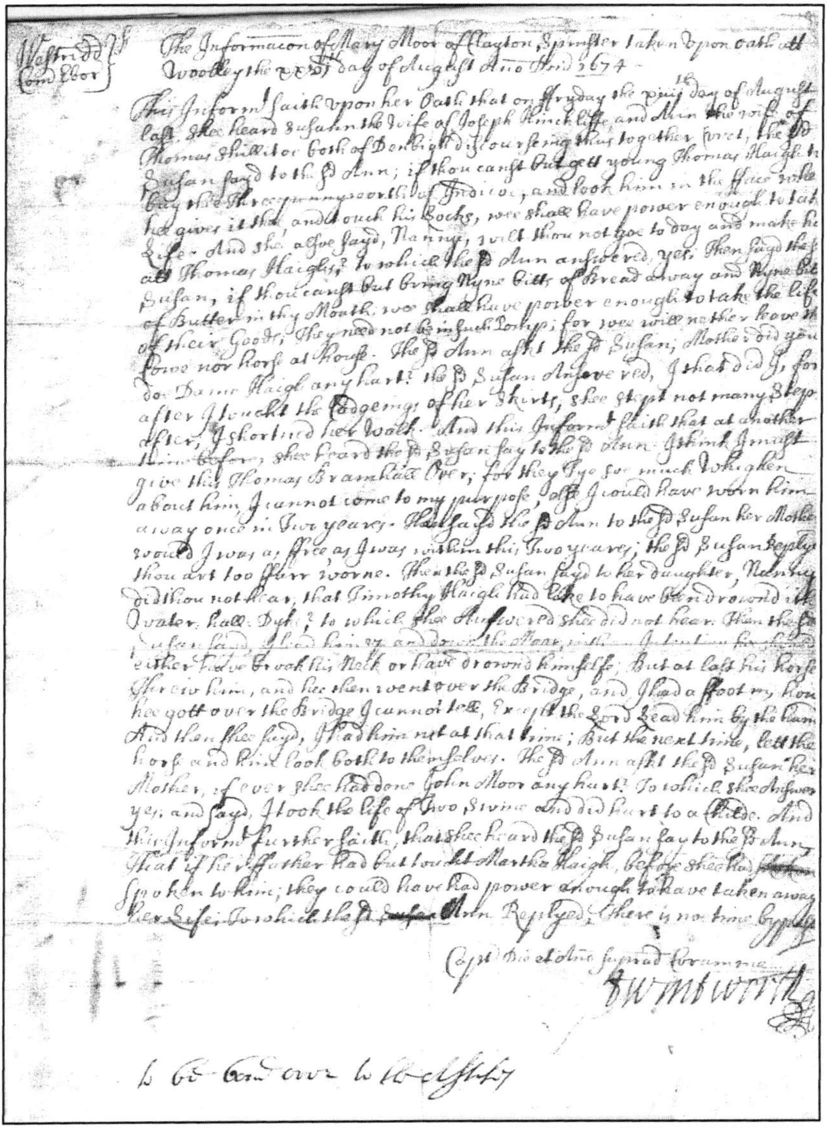

Fig. 8. **The deposition of Mary Moor, sworn at Woolley on 26 August, 1674.**
(National Archives ASSI 45/11/1 C321432)

By prefacing Haigh's name with the word "young", Moor's description of the accused's potential victim gives some idea of where he fitted in within the local community. Contemporary C17th records, such as Adam Eyre's diaries, evidence the practice of using "young" and "old", not as a means of identifying age, but more usually as a means of distinguishing between two members of a family with exactly the same first name. The Hearth Tax returns, a couple of years before the allegations were made, evidence a "Thomas Haigh" occupying what had probably been quite a sizeable property in Denby.[70] As a later allegation refers to a question about going "…to make hay at Thomas Haigh's?", it can probably be assumed this was a farmhouse and Chris Heath has suggested it was likely to have been located close to the site of the former Wagon and Horses public house, in Lower Denby, where the Haigh family had lived for generations.[71] The Denby with Clayton West Enclosure Map of 1802 notes significant landholdings by the Haighs in the Lower Denby area but John Haigh's occupation of Over Bagden as far back as 1604 has already been noted. In the context of the comments on haymaking at the Haighs, the deposition also makes clear that, while "Nanny" might, during the following century, have been used as a pet form of Nancy,[72] according to Moor's statement, it appears to have been what Susanna Hinchliffe called her daughter, Anne.

Moor speaks, as well, of the two women having dealings with a Thomas Bramhall, who seems to have been specially protected against witch influence by wearing what is termed "whigen." George Redmonds' glossary of Yorkshire words makes specific reference to the 1674 case in explaining this spelling as a variant of wiggen, quicken or whicken, the mountain ash or rowan, considered to fend off evil spirits.[73] It seems the John Moor also referred to – and most likely the complainant's father – may have been devoid of such protective cover as her deposition quotes Hinchliffe saying that, in his case, "I took the life of two swine and did hurt to a child." It is impossible to establish if John Moor had lost swine and had a child hurt in some way at the time. But evil influences might have offered a convenient explanation as to the cause of misfortune which could not be otherwise understood. The loss of family livestock and some possible harm to a sibling may have also had some bearing on Mary Moor's apparent grievances.

Another Haigh – Timothy – features, as well, in Mary Moor's deposition, when she alleges overhearing Hinchliffe say to Shillitoe that he had almost drowned in what appears to me to be called Quaker Hall dyke. Previous accounts of this deposition by Fred Lawton and Chris Heath[74] have concluded that this reference was actually to "Water Hall dyke" which could have meant the River Don, as it flows adjacent to Water Hall in Penistone. Certainly, both Susanna Hinchliffe and Timothy Haigh may have passed close to Water Hall on their way, perhaps, to Penistone Church. But it is doubtful that, even back in 1674, the Don would have been described as a mere ditch or water channel and this location was also some considerable distance from the areas where both Hinchliffe and Haigh seem to have inhabited, at a time, of course, when the Hinchliffes are more likely to have worshipped at Denby.

The suggestion seems to be that Hinchliffe had caused Haigh to ride his horse "…up and down the moor with an intention that he should either have broken his neck or have drowned himself." Where Quaker Hall dyke was is uncertain, but Bower and Knight's account of the origins of the Quakers of Wooldale, High Flatts and Midhope offers a possible clue. "Tradition states that meetings started to be held during the Commonwealth period (1649-1660) in a barn which is on the site of the present meeting house"[75] in High Flatts. As with Lower Denby's Papist Hall, the term "Quaker Hall" may have originally been used as a somewhat derogatory local reference to the religious connections of the location. What is now known as Munchcliffe Beck flows north east from near the High Flatts Meeting House, down through Munchcliffe Woods to Denby Dale and seems the most likely candidate to have been the Quaker Hall dyke of 1674. Moor's deposition speaks of a bridge over the dyke and, although, it is difficult to date its origins, there is a small stone bridge over

Munchcliffe Beck, close to its source, which carries a footway running east from the Meeting House towards Bank Lane in Upper Denby.

Fig. 9. Bridge over Munchcliffe Beck, near High Flatts Quaker Meeting House. (D. Hinchliffe).

Munchcliffe is a name with no apparent local connection whatsoever and Chris Heath has drawn attention to a 1607 document recording the disposal of some freehold land, which may offer some idea of its origin. It refers to "several parcels of common known as 'Cliffe' or 'Harcliffe' within the lordships or townships of Cumberworth and Denbie…"[76] But this source offers no explanation of how the 'Munch' element originated and it is open to question whether this name began as either a mispronunciation or misspelling of Hinchliffe or

30

Hinchcliffe. The Beck leads to Munchcliffe Wood. Although there could conceivably be a connection with the witchcraft case, because the wood is near to Hartcliffe Mills at Denby Dale, it is probably more likely to be linked with the textile company, Z. Hinchliffe and Sons, who have been based there since 1850. An alternative theory for the etymology of Munchcliffe, which does not seem to appear on any older maps, is that is yet another example of the C19th Ordnance Survey, misunderstanding a local name. As David Hey has explained, "The surveyors from the south of England did not always catch what the locals said to them."[77]

Moor claimed she heard Hinchliffe tell Shillitoe that if Anne's father "...had but touched Martha Haigh before she had spoken to him, they could have had power enough to take away her life." One account of the case erroneously suggests this involved "... the bewitching to death..."[78] of the victim but this claim does not appear in the relevant deposition. The likelihood is that Martha was from a different Haigh family to that headed by Thomas in Denby. The Penistone records note the baptism of a Martha, daughter of Gulielmi Haigh during 1651, and the marriage of a Martha Haigh to a Francis Haigh in 1676. Francis was probably the resident of Thurlstone recorded in the 1672 Hearth Tax returns, along with five other Haigh households in the township.[79] Whether this Martha was the woman referred to by Moor is difficult to confirm and what might have motivated the deliberations concerning her demise is impossible to fathom.

The strong likelihood of the key players in this affair having been involved in weaving is suggested by another of Mary Moor's allegations, where she referred to what Shillitoe supposedly said to Hinchliffe when Moor had gone to borrow a linewheel from them around the middle of July, 1674. Line (or lyne) would have been the fibre of flax, with the thread spun on a special linewheel. The finished cloth was also often known as line and there are references to this feature in local records both before and after the Denby case.[80] This deposition is dated 2 October, 1674, over a month after Moor's sworn statement before Wentworth at Woolley had led to the women being bound over to the Assizes. Her giving significant additional information at this point, to a different magistrate by the name of Blythman, does raise the question as to whether she was, by then, under some pressure over her role in the affair and felt the need to strengthen or embellish the claims.

This later deposition by Moor read: *This informant saith that about ye middle of July last past, going to borrow a linewheel she heard Ann Shillito say to Susan Hinchliffe (her mother) I saw my father play such a trick last night as I never saw in my life. Susan Hinchliffe asked Ann Shillito what yt was. Susan said he asked for butter and there came butter on to his knee in a wooden saucer. Susan said that it was but a little. Has thou lived in this house for so long and never saw none of thy father's tricks. Dost not thou know that thy father went to John Walker's to steime a pare of shoes and he would not let him have them without he had money in his hand, but he never made pare after. Likewise he went to George Copleys to steime a waistcoat cloth, and he would not let him have it without he had silver in his hand, and because he would not let him have it he never made a piece after it, but two. Susan Hinchliffe further said to Ann Shillito yt if anybody would not let them have what they wanted they could take life of anybody.*

This informant further saith yt she heard Susan Hinchliffe say to Ann Shillito yt Joseph Hinchliffe was as ill as they but would not be seen in it; he bore it far off. Ann Shillito further saith yt if they were known they might be hanged but Susan Hinchliffe replied no hemp would hang them; but Ann Shillito said they might be burnt then, Susan Hinchliffe said nay, they would never tell until they died.

This informant further saith yt upon ye twentieth of September Ann Shillito said I'll warrant yt thou shall but say little when thou comes before the bench.

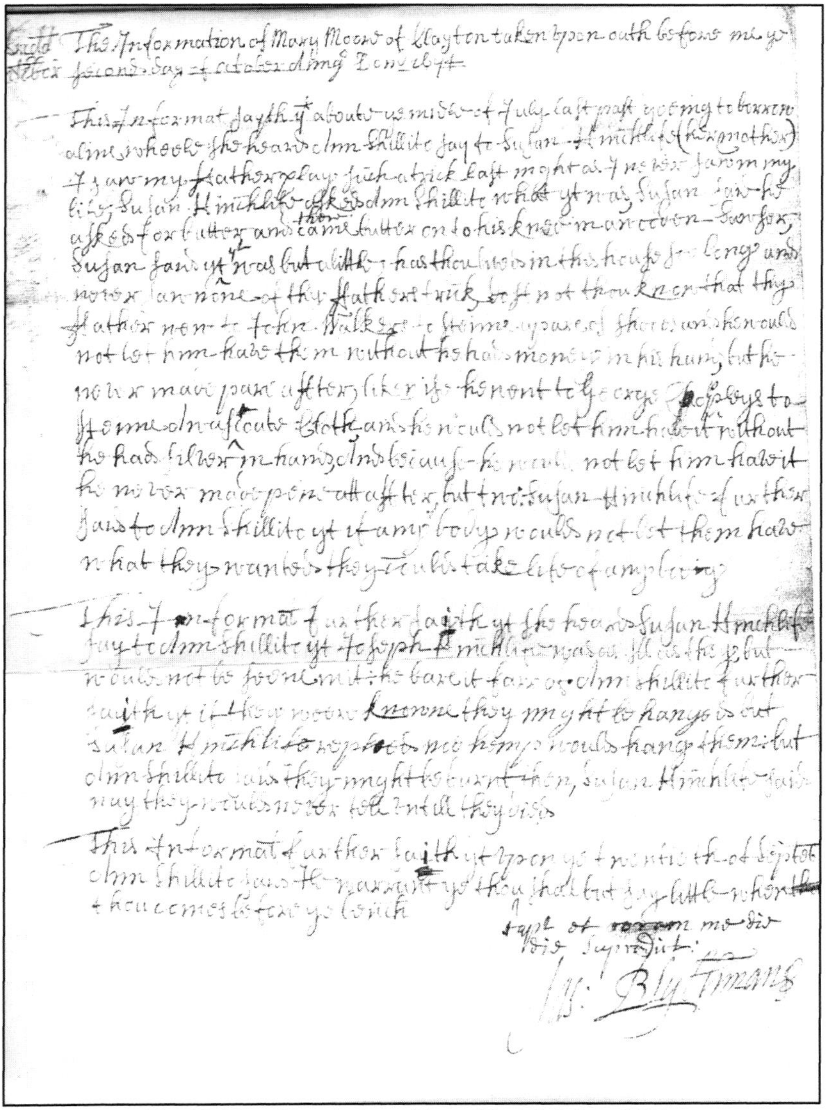

Fig. 10. Mary Moor's deposition of 2nd October, 1674.
(National Archives ASSI 45/11/1 C32143)

Moor seems to have been suggesting that Susanna Hinchliffe was, at the time, telling Shillitoe of the detail of some of her father's "tricks", such as – apparently – producing butter on his knee in a wooden saucer. She quotes Susanna outlining her husband's dealings with a John Walker over his 'steime' or order for a pair of shoes, with Walker refusing to supply them until Joseph Hinchliffe had the money. Susanna had supposedly suggested her husband's "tricks" had meant that shoe-maker Walker – probably of Kexbrough[81]- never produced another pair. Susanna allegedly credited Joseph with a similar sanction against George Copley, from whom he had ordered waist coat cloth. Again, the refusal to supply in advance of payment meant Copley, most likely a resident of Flockton,[82] only ever produced two more pieces, according to Moor's account of the mother and daughter discussion. The final point in the initial paragraph of the deposition has Moor making the most serious allegation that Susanna Hinchliffe was clearly claiming they had the power to take life.

It is difficult to establish if Moor's claim that Susanna Hinchliffe referred to her husband being "as ill as they were" bore any relationship to the family's actual health although, in the mother's case, subsequent evidence did come to light that her general well being may have been poor. The concluding claims from Moor imply that Hinchliffe and Shillitoe were clearly cognisant of the fact that they may face their deaths as a consequence of their situation.

It is hard to know whether to deem it significant or bizarre that an additional deposition concerning this case contains allegations possibly relating to the accuser herself, which were put to a different magistrate from those dealing with Hinchliffe and Shillitoe, by the name of Osborne. The same Timothy Haigh testified on 15 October, 1674, to seeing Mary Moor vomit bended wire and a piece of paper containing two crooked pins, mentioning other occasions she had vomited pins. The possibility of Timothy being 'young' Thomas Haigh's brother has been raised earlier. With this Thomas quite likely to have been the eldest son of the Denby farmer – and named after him – the question is again raised as to Timothy's age. If there was any basis whatsoever to Moor's statements concerning Susanna Hinchliffe leading him on a horse, might it be safely assumed he was of a young age and, if so, under what circumstances was this deposition obtained?

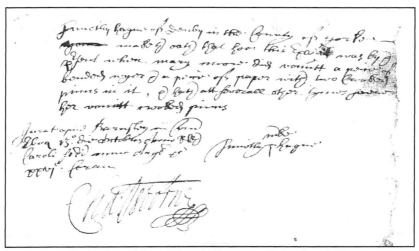

Fig. 11. Deposition of Timothy Hague on 15 October, 1674.
(National Archives ASSI 45/11/1 C321432)

Any examination of the 1674 case has to consider the defence mounted in support of the accused and, perhaps, question whether, in making these claims, Timothy Haigh came under pressure from what might be termed the 'defence' side to point a finger at Moor and her own, rather odd, alleged behaviour. Did he resent being a key party to the Moor allegations and the focus of what would have been considerable attention locally as a direct result of the case? Or was what Haigh stated he had seen deemed additional evidence of the influence of the accused over Moor? But, if he had actually seen Moor 'vomit' these pins, was there an innocent explanation to what he had witnessed? We know the likelihood of her involvement in some capacity in the weaving trade. Even in contemporary times, it is not unknown to see those involved in craft work keeping pins and other items in their mouths when their hands are otherwise occupied. Had Haigh witnessed an entirely harmless act which had been completely misinterpreted as having malign intent? Was a young lad's account of what he had seen seized upon and deliberately skewed in an effort to either discredit Moor or increase the pressure on Hinchliffe and Shillitoe?

An alternative explanation concerning pins featuring in his testament is the likely folk memory of the remarkable events which had unfolded half a century earlier in what became known as the Pendle witch trials, arising from malefic allegations on the other side of the Pennines. There is a distinct possibility that Haigh and others may have had some knowledge of the quite central role expensive metal pins had played in the series of cases which gained national prominence. What has been described as a "spark" setting tensions around witchcraft alight[83] had occurred on 18 March, 1612, when Alizon Device, a local beggar, was alleged to have approached elderly Halifax pedlar, John Law, who was travelling near Colne, in north east Lancashire, selling luxuries. She asked him for pins which he refused to give her and, after she had supposedly cursed him, he had fallen to the ground. One account suggests that "...by the time he managed to reach a nearby inn, John Law was completely lame down one side of the body."[84]What had been probably a stroke was deemed evidence of bewitching, with the belief that such pins could be used for magical purposes strengthening the subsequent case against Device.

The likelihood that Timothy Haigh's testament may well have been intended as additional evidence of the accused's malefic powers is strengthened by another deposition in the name of Elizabeth Brooke of Clayton, again sworn before the third magistrate, Osborne. In it she is described as a "spinster aged sixty years or thereabouts..." who "...being a near neighbour..." had called in on Mary Moor. [85] The plaintiff had detailed to her the lengthy account of vomiting pins and it would appear Brooke had also seen her do it.

But the deposition claimed Brooke had put her fingers in Moor's mouth to ascertain there were no pins in it before she was seen to vomit them. The witness's mark is appended at the conclusion of her statement[86]

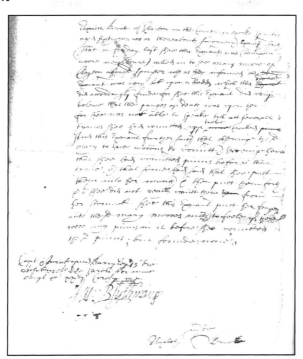

Fig. 12. Deposition of Elizabeth Brooke, of Clayton.
(National Archives ASSI 45/11/1 C321432)

We are left with another possibility, of course, that what Haigh and Brooke described could have actually been an honest account of what they recalled seeing, with Mary Moor being engaged in some form of self-harm. There is a rare psychiatric disorder, most commonly noted in teenage girls or young women, involving the ingestion of sharp items. Do these two depositions raise the possibility that Moor had issues with her mental health?

5. Due Process?

In an age of widespread illiteracy, it was local word of mouth that passed news from community to community, with more significant events being announced from the pulpit of the parish church on Sundays. The likelihood is that it was gossip between local folk in Clayton, Denby and the wider Penistone parish, which led to the 1674 allegations gaining the traction needed to see them being apparently taken seriously within the judicial process of the time.

It is, perhaps, not difficult to feel rather sorry for the person whose role meant he was the potential first port of call in a system hardly designed to deal with the issues arising from Moor's allegations about Hinchliffe and Shillitoe. The local parish constable was a very different being from our modern police officer and would have been less than pleased to find himself in the midst of a serious local altercation which had developed following the controversial claims of a teenage girl. The role of constable was originally that of a formal bond between the ancient lord of the manor and their tenants, appointed by and reporting to the local court leets on minor matters of law and order. By the time of the Denby case, constables were increasingly appointed by parish vestry meetings and, within larger parishes, like Penistone, assigned on a township basis.

The Denby appointment would have been an annual one, with no payment received by the constable and no compensation for the impact of the role on any loss of earnings from their usual occupation. He had powers of arrest under common law as a "conservator of the peace"[87] and was responsible to the local Justices of the Peace for these aspects of the role. In an aside on the many challenges of the constable's work, David Hey could – unknowingly – have very much hit the 1674 nail on the head in writing of the dilemmas faced. "Most troubles were dealt with informally or by arbitration, but a constable could find himself in situations where his responsibilities to the Justices of the Peace conflicted with a communal sense of good neighbourliness."[88]

The first major law setting out detailed procedures to deal with witchcraft was enacted in 1563, during the reign of Elizabeth I. However, the powers which would have underpinned the action being taken in 1674 are likely to have stemmed from later legislation, passed under James I in 1604, which was to provide the legal framework for most of the subsequent witchcraft trials. This Act significantly strengthened the sanctions available to the courts and the fact that the death penalty could subsequently be used where injury occurred through witchcraft would have clearly added to concerns around the Denby case.

Quite how this matter may have come to the local constable's attention is not obvious from the materials which survive from the episode, but his awareness of the allegations is likely to have arisen directly as a consequence of the extent to which they were clearly debated vigorously in the locality and, as will be noted later, very evidently divided opinion. There would have been widespread knowledge of the seriousness of the allegations being made against Hinchliffe and Shillitoe beyond just Upper and Lower Denby and Moor's home village of Clayton.

The surviving records of the affair and, in particular, the sworn depositions, indicate that matters were placed in the hands of a local Justice of the Peace, most likely by the Denby constable, during the summer of 1674. The occupants of these magistrates' roles had, from their origins during medieval times, usually come from landowning gentry. Jack Binns' detailed account of C17th Yorkshire notes that "Justices had to be county residents and possess freehold property worth at least £20 a year, though in practice their incomes were considerably more than this."[89] The 300 or so JPs operating within the old West Riding at this time undertook a whole range of administrative decision-making, alongside their judicial function and were the local 'ruling class' both before, during and after the Civil War.

As we have noted, the most serious allegations were contained in a statement made on oath by Moor in front of a magistrate at

Woolley, near Wakefield, on 26 August that year. Sometimes called sessions papers, indicating their likely court use, such depositions recorded pre-trial witness testimonies. This one was detailed, lengthy and clearly signed by a Wentworth, although exactly which member of which branch of this Yorkshire dynasty is not entirely clear. The Surtees Society record of the case, from 1861, suggests it was heard by "Darcy Wentworth at Woolley"[90] and local Skelmanthorpe historian, Fred Lawton, similarly asserted many years ago that it was him who had dealt with the case,[91] as did Barnsley antiquarian, Eli Hoyle.[92] Others writing about it in more recent times have endorsed this account[93] but Eileen Rennison, in her detailed examination of numerous 'witchcraft' allegations in Yorkshire, qualified his identity as "Henry Darcy Wentworth."[94] None of those who have previously written about this episode have revealed how they came to their identification of the key magistrate dealing with the allegations but, bearing in mind the document concludes with the words "To be bound over to Assizes", establishing exactly who they were is crucially important to an understanding of the case.

To this day, Woolley has a property known as the Old Court House, built originally as a farmhouse in 1642, which allegedly "spent time as a local prison and boasts a tunnel leading from the cellar to nearby Woolley Hall, a legacy from its English Civil War origins." [95] The Moor deposition is quite clear that it was in this village where she gave the evidence and, with one branch of the Wentworths being longstanding residents of Woolley Hall, the likelihood is that this was where it was actually sworn. The complication in terms of identifying the actual magistrate is that a Darcy does not seem to feature in any lineage of the Wentworths at this location and an adult member of the wider family of this name is impossible to identify around the time of the Denby case.

Written in 1831, Joseph Hunter's "South Yorkshire" has extensive pedigrees for branches of the Wentworths, from those originally using that name in Wath-upon-Dearne, to other locations including North & South Elmsall, Brodsworth, and Bretton, as well as Woolley.

Fig. 13. A 20th century image of Woolley Hall, which had been enlarged and altered during the late 17th and early 18th centuries.
(Courtesy of Wakefield Express)

Hunter advised that "Winteworth" was "still the pronunciation of the name, whether of the place or of the family, by the common people, who do not easily fall into new modes of speech." In endeavouring to put forward suggestions for the origins and make-up of the surname, he suggested that "The latter half of the name is one of the most frequent local terminals, and appears to note some degree of cultivation. The former half affords room for conjecture."[96] The references to "common people" and "cultivation" perhaps provide a contrast which would have been even more marked in 1674 when those involved as plaintiffs, witnesses and defendants found themselves in front of the Wentworth Justice of the Peace at Woolley.

The name "Darcy" features primarily within the branch of the Wentworths located, during the 16th and 17th centuries, at Brodsworth, to the north-west of Doncaster. The first use of this first name seems to be in 1592 when it was given to the younger son of Thomas Wentworth of South Kirkby and his wife, who came from the

Goodrick family of Ribston, near Knaresborough, in north Yorkshire. Hunter has outlined this Darcy Wentworth's involvement with his family in the governance of Ireland and notes that, perhaps surprisingly, "At the commencement of the civil wars he appears to have sided with the parliament."[97] The nobility did not necessarily retain their allegiances so it may be unwise to place too much emphasis on him being apparently at odds with most of the other Wentworths in these affiliations. While he had returned to Brodsworth after the restoration of the monarchy, he was dead by 1667, some years before the Denby case.

Darcy Wentworth had died without issue, leaving the Brodsworth estate to his nephew, Henry Wentworth. The name "Darcy" was continued with Henry naming two of his four sons after his uncle. One of them clearly predeceased the other and neither of them appears to have survived into adulthood. But the occupant of Woolley Hall is clearly recorded shortly before the case, in 1672, as "John Wentworth Esqr"[98] and the Hearth Tax returns of that year note the involvement of a Justice of the Peace by the name of "J. Wentworth" in what is likely to have been the ratification of certificates of exemption for the poor in nearby Barnsley, Worsborough and Staincross.[99]

If, as seems likely, these two were one and the same, some consideration of John's background may offer possible insights into why the 1674 allegations were apparently handled in the way they were. He was the fifth son of Michael Wentworth and his wife, Frances (nee Downes). Michael had come to Woolley in 1599, purchasing the estate from the Woodrove family. A staunch Catholic, he had a private chapel at the Hall, and the Woolley Wentworths' family archive held at Leeds University offers evidence that Frances shared his faith. Around the time of John's birth, in 1605, his father had made a payment of the then substantial sum of £180 in respect of Frances' recusancy.[100] John inherited the Woolley estate on the death of his older brother, Sir George Wentworth, in 1666. Sir George had been a colonel in a regiment of foot opposing Parliament during the Civil Wars, has been described as among "...the nucleus of Yorkshire's Royalist party,"[101] and was among those forced into Pontefract Castle during Christmas of 1644 when Parliamentary forces occupied the nearby town.[102] In marked contrast to his father, Sir George was a Protestant and allegedly used the private chapel as a wood store following Michael's death.[103]

Jack Binns' account of Civil War Yorkshire makes clear that, although Sir George's composition for supporting Charles I was, according to his own account "...the greatest fine that hath been set upon any beyond Trent,"[104] his coal mining interests and later acquisition of land from other Royalist estates meant that his brother's wealth was substantial. One account of Sir George's fine suggests it was £3,188, while John's was a 'mere' £70.[105] John Wentworth's Civil War profile was clearly not on a par with Sir George's distinguished service in the Royalist cause, but it is not unreasonable to believe he shared the same political sympathies.

Both Sir George and John were, of course, the cousins of Sir Thomas Wentworth, later the Earl of Strafford, who had been very close to Charles I and a key figure in the build up to the Civil War, until his execution in May, 1641. Strafford, himself, had written from the Tower of London to the King, urging him to sign his death warrant in the hope that his execution would appease Charles' many enemies. It is clear that the King bitterly regretted his treatment of Strafford saying, at his own execution in 1649, that "...he was paying the price for his betrayal of a good and loyal man."[106] Dugdale's Visitation of Yorkshire describes John Wentworth as "bred a lawyer" and notes his role as Secretary to his cousin[107]. Strafford had been a staunch Protestant but a significant proportion of the Yorkshire gentry, both before and during that conflict, were by contrast of the Catholic faith. In his detailed analysis of C17th Yorkshire gentry, J. T. Cliffe suggested that, among the 679 families in the county he was able to pinpoint, over 300 were wholly or in part Catholics.[108] Of the 157 families supporting Catholicism in their entirety, some 86 were to become

Royalists in the Civil War, 10 become Parliamentarians, while the rest stayed neutral.[109]

The precise religious outlook of John Wentworth is not clear but we must assume that, by the time of the Denby case, he had taken the oaths of allegiance and signed the declarations required of a civil office holder under the provisions of the 1673 Test Act. This legislation, passed, along with subsequent laws, because of concerns over popish plots, required the likes of justices of the peace and military officeholders to formally denounce key doctrines of Catholicism. Nevertheless, given his family background within that faith, it has to be asked whether Wentworth might have been what was known at the time as a 'Church Papist'. This derogatory term was applied to English Catholics who ostensibly followed the Protestant religion but retained a personal belief in Roman Catholicism.[110]

It would appear that John Wentworth had previously served alongside another local magistrate who was also involved in taking evidence relating to the witchcraft allegations. Rowland Jackson's 1858 history of Barnsley records that, sitting with Wentworth at a special session regarding "oppression by the poor", in Barnsley, on 10 October, 1671, was Jasper Blythman.[111] He was responsible for, firstly, the sworn witness statement by Elizabeth Brooke, Mary Moor's neighbour in Clayton, which was probably taken during August of 1674. But Blythman also took directly from Moor the sworn statement relating to John Walker and George Copley which was dated 2 October, 1674,[112] more than a month after Wentworth had bound the accused over to the Assizes.

Like Wentworth, Jasper Blythman came from markedly different stock to the Denby plaintiff and accused. He had attended Sedbergh School and, according to their records, went on to enter St John's College, Cambridge in 1661, at the age of 19. He was the third son of William Blythman, described as of Royston,[113] near Barnsley, and Elizabeth Stanhope, but is later noted by Sedbergh School as being of "Newlay, Leeds."[114] The Blythman (or Blithman) name featured among Yorkshire officialdom from at least the time of the dissolution of the monasteries, with Jackson stating that an earlier William Blithman was one of the commissioners who was "...taking the surrenders, and dissolvyd the monasteries..."including at Tickhill and Monk Bretton on 15 December, 1537.[115]

Jasper Blythman's father featured on a number of occasions in the Civil War diaries of Hazlehead''s Adam Eyre, when he and Ralph Wordsworth, of Water Hall, Penistone, had extensive contact with William concerning funding for Penistone Church and the difficulties relating to the attempted removal of the vicar, Christopher Dickenson, who had been accused of drunkenness and other behaviours unbecoming of his office. That contact appears to have involved them in travelling over to what is noted as "New Lathes" on a number of occasions during 1647.[116] The diaries contain an explanatory note to the effect that "William Blythman of New Laith, Esq., had been an active Royalist, and had to compound for his estates." This payment, probably in lieu of a prosecution for his opposition to the Parliamentary cause, included a requirement to give financial support towards the maintenance of the minister at Penistone Church[117] and Dransfield suggested it required him paying what would then have been the sizeable amount of £50 per annum, over a 26-year period.[118]

While Jasper Blythman seems, from the Sedbergh School records, to have had early family connections in the Leeds area and was later to serve in the role of Recorder for Leeds, it is likely that, at the time of his involvement with the 1674 case, he was living within what is nowadays known as South Yorkshire. On 4 November, 1663, Blythman had married Katherine Mountney (or Mountenry) in Rotherham. The West Riding Hearth Tax returns, less than a decade later, offer no record of any Blythmans by that time at Newlay but record three separate entries for a "Mr Blythman" closer to where Jasper and Elizabeth had married. Two are noted – with seven and four hearths respectively – in Carlton, between Royston and Barnsley, and a third – with eight – in Swinton, between Rotherham and Doncaster.[119] This latter location seems the most likely residence for the magistrate in 1674.

The final member of this magisterial triumvirate had the surname of Osborne and witnessed the deposition of "Timothy Hague" of Denby, which is signed off with Hague's mark. The spelling of the surname is clearly a variant of the Haigh featured in Moor's main deposition. As with John Wentworth, there is evidence of the involvement of a Charles Osborne, Justice of the Peace, in witnessing exemption certificates within South Yorkshire during the compilation of the Hearth Tax returns in 1672,[120] and the initial in the deposition signature does appear to be a 'C'.[121]

It seems that he, too, had an interesting pedigree, being the second son of Sir Edward Osborne, of Kiverton, and his second wife, Anne Walmesley. Like Wentworth and Blythman, Charles Osborne came from strong Royalist stock, his father – an MP variously for East Retford, Berwick and York – being vice-president of the Council of the North and a staunch supporter of Charles I. Sir Thomas Osborne, Charles' brother, was the first Duke of Leeds and has been described as "...a personal friend of Charles II."[122] Subsequently, Thomas was a conspirator against James II and involved in the plan to invite William of Orange to take the English throne. As Governor of Hull, Thomas was influential in securing the election of his brother, Charles, as a Hull MP in the Tory cause in 1690.[123]

One account of the Denby case maintains that in the late summer of 1674, prior to the referral of their case to the Assizes, the two accused women had "...found themselves locked in a Barnsley gaol..." on the witchcraft charge.[124] Bearing in mind that Joseph Hinchliffe was clearly implicated, as well, in some of the depositions on the case, it is interesting that it seems that the initial allegations against him were not apparently pursued. The testimonies upon which the case was based appear to point more to his alleged 'powers' than the involvement of his daughter, but it was Shillitoe who, with her mother, is accused. Some 90% of witchcraft cases reaching the English Assizes involved women, so did the handling of the Denby case by these male magistrates reflect what has been argued to be one aspect of the male domination of women?[125]

The Yorkshire area was within what was known as the Northern Assize Circuit during this part of the C17th and the allegations began to progress within the judicial system around the time the summer Assize hearings would have been already underway or concluding. The option of some sort of magisterial remand, either in custody or within the community, was possible as a consequence of John Wentworth's binding over the case for hearing at the Lent or Spring Assizes, to be held during the following March or April. However, it is the Timothy Hague deposition – signed by Charles Osborne – which is the only extant legal document seeming to make an explicit reference to Barnsley. But the Latin term *Iuratoris* preceeding mention of the location and Osborne's signature would most likely seem to just indicate that Hague swore the deposition in front of the magistrate in Barnsley.

Despite then having just chapel-of-ease status for St. Mary's Church within the Silkstone parish, it is known that Barnsley did have a prison facility at the time of the Denby case. Its function is likely to have been limited to that of a temporary holding facility pending, usually, the payment of some form of debt or the accused's appearance at the Quarter Sessions or Assizes. Gerald Alliott has described how what were known as 'grates' held the prisoners and suggested this term is likely to have arisen because of the small aperture in the door through which those held could be both observed and fed.[126] The Moot Hall, which was situated near the top of Market Hill in Barnsley, was the location for the Quarter Sessions and the oldest of the grates, which was used until the early 1800s, was located below it.[127]

We have no proof whatsoever that the Denby accused were held here but it is known that, where those accused of witchcraft were held in custodial settings, the conditions they had to endure were often a good deal more severe than those faced by other prisoners. David and Andrew Pickerings' analysis of witch persecution in

England makes the point that, because of the perception they had "diabolical powers", alleged witches were likely to be held in much more secure conditions. They quote a contemporary report of the treatment of Anne Foster who faced similar claims during the same year as the Denby case. "No sooner was she brought in, but the keepers of the (Northampton) Gaol caused her to be chained to a post that was in the Gaol."[128]

6. The petition (i): an issue of popular scepticism

A common theme in the recounting of witchcraft allegations is often the extent to which a local community would frequently turn against the accused in what might be described as a form of mass hysteria. But, in his account of witchcraft in early modern England, James Sharpe cautions against this notion which, he suggests, ignores what he terms "...the issue of popular scepticism."[129] He includes, in his detailed account of the persecutions, reference to the Hinchliffe and Shillitoe case as an important illustration "...of how witchcraft accusations might be contested locally."[130]

The particular historical significance of the Denby allegations of 1674 is the fact that a petition of over fifty local residents was drawn up in support of the accused, strongly testifying to their good character. An examination of the signatures it contains – as far as this is possible accurately – opens a remarkable window into the relationships, functioning and thinking of a considerable number who were living nearby at the time. It is, obviously, important to note that at this point in our history and through to the late C19th, a significant proportion of the population were totally illiterate, leaving their 'marks' – often a simple cross – in documents such as parish marriage registers. There are no 'marks' of those unable to sign their names on this petition so it does reflect the thoughts of those probably better educated and largely of a higher social status than the accused. It was later to be argued that the petitioners could be regarded as 'decent' folk. Writing at the very start of the C20th, local Skelmanthorpe historian, Fred Lawton, suggested that "Many respectable names appear on it,"[131] and also penning his thoughts around the same time, Barnsley's Eli Hoyle concurred that they were "... of a respectable class."[132] It could, arguably, be termed a remarkable roll call of a large number of the local great and good, united, as can be seen in many cases, by a not dissimilar religious and political outlook.

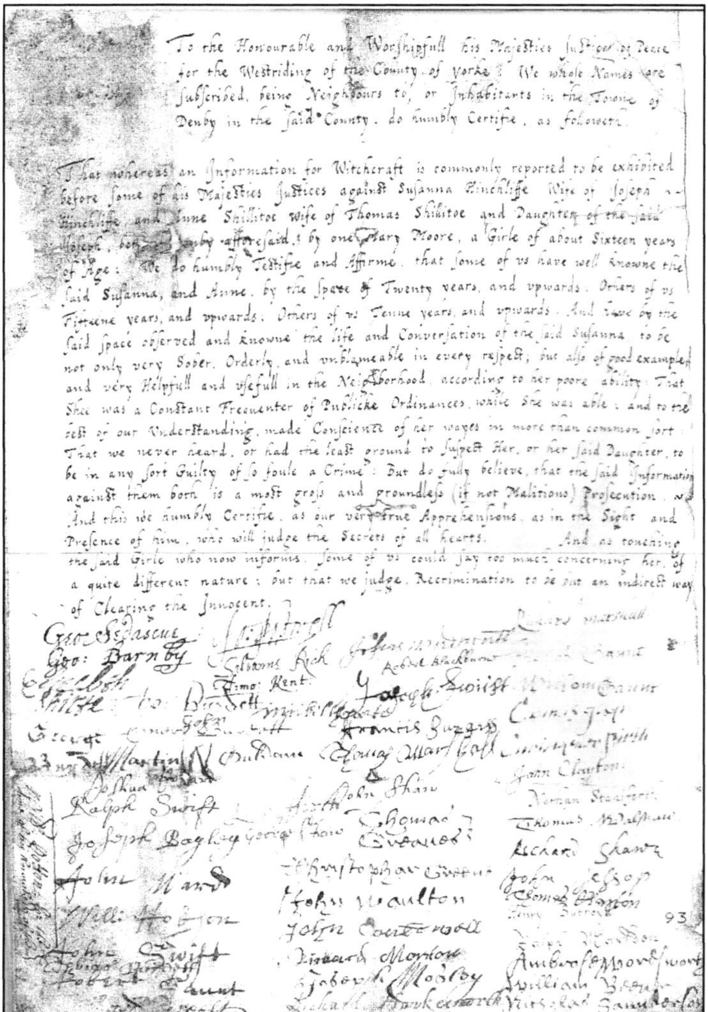

Fig. 14. The formal petition in support of the accused, presented to the magistrates. (National Archives ASSI 45/11/1 C321432)

It is more than fortunate that the Assize records held by National Archives relating to this case contain the original copy of this petition[133] so it is possible to examine its detailed wording and establish from it the actual, or in other instances, likely identity of its supporters. The preamble to the detailed wording of it gives a clear idea of who it was to be presented to and a broad description of how the signatories saw themselves relating to the case:

To the Honourable and Worshipfull his Majesties Justices of Peace for the Westriding of the County of Yorke. We whose names are subscribed, being Neighbours to, or Inhabitants in the Towne of Denby in the said County, do humbly certifie, as followeth.

Firstly, it is clear from who the petition is addressed to that, although it appears undated, it was drawn up around the time the allegations had been placed in the hands of the three magistrates involved, during the summer and early Autumn of 1674. It makes representations specifically to the Justices of the Peace, who we know to have been Wentworth, Blythman and Osborne, so it clearly predates a referral of the case for an Assize hearing. Secondly, it specifies that the signatories were either "neighbours to, or inhabitants in the Towne of Denby". Like a number of other large Pennine parishes, Penistone was subdivided into townships and Denby constituted one of them, so we know that many of the petitioners – like the accused – resided in the area.

But, to understand the identities of others supporting Hinchliffe and Shillitoe, we perhaps need to appreciate that the term 'neighbours' during the 17th century meant a little more than those living just a few doors away. The diaries of Adam Eyre, recording life within Penistone parish a couple of decades earlier, evidence that his life was shared with many folk outside his family who lived a considerable distance from his home who he would have regarded as his 'neighbours'.[134] As will be clear when the habitations of the signatories are looked at, a number of these 'neighbours' lived quite some way from what might be termed the scenes of the alleged 'crime'.

The content of the petition is, fortunately, clearly readable and needs to be noted in its entirety in order to fully appreciate the detailed concerns being expressed by its supporters:

That whereas an Information for Witchcraft is commonly reported to be exhibited before some of his Majesties Justices against Susanna Hinchliffe Wife of Joseph Hinchliffe, and Anne Shillitoe Wife of Thomas Shillittoe and Daughter of the said Joseph, both of Denby aforesaid, by one Mary Moore, a Girle of about Sixteen years of Age. We do humbly Testifie and Affirme, that some of us have well knowne the said Susanna, and Anne, by the space of Twenty years, and upwards. And have by the said space observed and known the life and Conversation of the said Susanna, to be not only very sober, orderly, and unblameable in every respect; but also of good example and very helpful and useful in the Neighbourhood, according to her poore ability. That shee was a Constant Frequenter of Publicke Ordinances, while she was able, and to the best of our Understanding, made Conscience of her ways in more than common sort. That we never heard, or had the least ground to suspect Her, or her said Daughter, to be in any sort Guilty of so foule a Crime. But do fully believe, that the said Information against them both is a most gross and groundless (if not Malitious) Prosecution. And we humbly Certifie, as our very true Apprehensions, as in the Sight and Presence of him, who will judge the Secrets of all our hearts. And as touching on the said Girle who now informs, some of us could say too much concerning her, of a quite different nature, but that we judge Recrimination to be but an indirect way of Clearing the Innocent.

The wording would appear to confirm that, by the time the petition was drawn up, Joseph Hinchliffe was no longer featuring alongside his wife and daughter as one of the accused. His only mentions in it relate to Susanna being his wife and Anne his daughter and the petitioners, by the time the signatures were being collected, were presumably then collectively of the view that there was no need to offer specific testimony in Joseph's support.

Some picture of Susanna Hinchliffe clearly emerges from how she is described in the petition's wording. We have already noted that she could well have been in late middle age by the time of the case and, like many older women of that era (and since), physically worn out by child-bearing during her fertile years and by a life of continual hard labour and struggle. The reference to her "poore ability" is much more likely to be confirmation of some physical illness or incapacity rather than intellectual limitations or low intelligence. The description of her as a "Constant Frequenter of Publicke Ordinances, while she was able..." seems to confirm Susanna as having been a regular churchgoer until that illness or incapacity meant she was no longer able to attend on the Sabbath. The suggestion that she "...made Conscience of her ways in more than common sort" perhaps implies a general belief that she tried to live her life in line with the religious principles subscribed to by many of the petitioners.

We cannot establish whether the full detail of the allegations contained in the various depositions which had been sworn by then would have been known to the petition's signatories but, even if they were aware of just a broad outline of the claims, it seems to have been sufficient for them to assert that the action being taken was "...a most gross and groundless (if not Malitious) Prosecution." They supply no detail of their grounds for implying this but clearly leave little doubt that what could be said of Mary Moor in terms of her character, was "of a quite different nature." The use of the term "recrimination" in the context of the concluding reference to her seems to suggest that at least some of those supporting Hinchliffe and Shillitoe may have been aware of some damaging information about Moor which they had chosen not to pass on.

Who initiated and organised the petition is not possible to establish with complete certainty, but the fact that the handwriting on its wording clearly matches one of the subsequent signatures attached points to one particular individual's involvement and perhaps gives an important indication of the outlook and beliefs of many of those backing the Denby women. The Reverend Nathan

Staniforth typified the sizeable number of churchmen of a Puritanical outlook who found themselves at the heart of some of the religious struggles playing out within parishes such as Penistone around the time of the Denby affair. David Hey's account of Penistone and district's history suggests that Staniforth had been "ejected from his living at Hognaston (Derbyshire)"[135] and presumably this was as a consequence of his unacceptable views. He features in both Hey's account and the earlier Penistone history by John Dransfield[136] as a key figure in the parish's past, occupying the roles of both parish clerk and the master of Penistone Grammar School. The School, probably located originally within St John the Baptist Church itself and later in the Kirk Flatt, close to its northern side, appears to have played an important role in drawing together support for the accused. Staniforth was central to this but it would be wrong to conclude that his involvement was confined to just putting the thoughts of the petitioners down on paper. Although he is known to have drawn up other important petitions in subsequent years,[137] the fact that he was also a signatory evidences that the initiative had the active support of some very influential local people.

Fig. 15. The old Grammar School, Penistone.
(Dransfield, 1906)

It is unlikely that the order in which the signatures appeared was anything other than random and a consequence of how it circulated among local parishioners, perhaps as and when they met. It is, in fact, difficult to describe any real order as, although they appear in what might be described as four separate columns, the names sometimes overlap, making the signatures difficult in some cases to decipher. All are horizontal on the petition document, other than one inserted – perhaps belatedly – in a vertical manner to the extreme left of the other names. From what is, in parts, quite a jumble, it is with difficulty, possible to identify what seems to be a total of some fifty-one signatures. From them, a significant number of the supporters of the accused can be clearly identified but a small number of those signing the petition remain something of a mystery. There is a Thomas Morton on it and that name is recorded in Cawthorne in 1672 but it is unclear if he is the same person. Cawthorne was, of course, outside the Penistone parish, as was Bradfield, where the name of a William Hobson, which appears on the petition, is noted at the same time. Both could have moved to live nearer the vicinity by the time the Denby case came to light but, as the wording of the petition speaks of the signatories being "...Neighbours to, or inhabitants in the Towne of Denby", their possible interest in the accusations should not be completely dismissed. The identities of the John Ward, Christopher Firth, Richard Morton and Henry Butroyd also signing the petition remain to be firmly established.

Deciphering all the names on the petition is not easy but the following appear to be on it:

George Sedescue	Jo: Sotwell	Josias Wordsworth
Richard Marshall	George Barnby	Silvanus Rich
Robert Blackburn	Thomas Gaunt	Elizabeth Shirt
Timo. Kent	Joseph Swift	William Gaunt
Thomas Burdett	Francis Burditt	Thomas Jessop
Emoria Burdett	Thomas Marshall	Christopher Firth
John Micklethwaite	John Shaw	John Clayton
George Burdett	George Firth	Nathan Staniforth
Joshua Pollard	George Shaw	Thomas Walshaw
Ralph Swift	Thomas Greaves	Richard Shaw
Joseph Bayley	Christopher Greene	John Jessop
John Ward	John Wallom	Thomas Morton
Willm Hobson	John Couldwell	Henry Butroyd
John Swift	Richard Morton	Ralph Marsden
Tobias Burdett	Joseph Mosley	Ambrose Wordsworth
Robert Gaunt	Richard Hawksworth	William Beever
Richard Prest	Nicholas Saunderson	
William Cotton (from the time of his knowledge of them)		

Fig. 16. The petition signatures.
(National Archives ASSI 45/11/1 C321432)

7. The petition (ii): venerable voices

The very first name at the top of the petition's left-hand column leads an impressive roll-call of those locals who'd had strong Parliamentary sympathies during the recent Civil Wars. George James Sedascue was the anglicised name of a major in Cromwell's army whose original appellation may have been Jan George Sadowski.[138] Dransfield suggests that this "...Lord's son in Germany..." had fled to England in 1640[139] but an earlier note in his Penistone history indicates that, fighting on behalf of the Elector Palatine, he had lost his estate following the Battle of Prague[140] which actually took place during the second half of 1648.

Sedascue was a Protestant Pole by origin but at the time of the 1648 battle, Prague was part of the Kingdom of Bohemia, an imperial state within the Holy Roman Empire. He subsequently became a naturalised Englishman through the passing of a private act of Parliament on 27 November, 1656. It is likely that, by then, Sedascue had distinguished himself within Oliver Cromwell's New Model Army, serving under Sir Thomas Fairfax. The House of Commons Journal covering proceedings for 11 January, 1660, includes a list of the names of the army officers appointed to serve under the Regiment of Horse, led by Colonel Crooke. It notes it was "Resolved that Major George Sedascue be Major of this Regiment, and Captain of a Troop in the same."[141] He was obviously a man of some influence and one analysis of the officer list of the New Model Army suggests that Sedascue may have been personally responsible for Cromwell's support for the Polish Protestants when they were threatened by a Catholic uprising.[142] Major Sedascue had married Mary, the daughter of fellow Parliamentary soldier, Colonel Godfrey Bosville, and was resident at the Bosville family home in Gunthwaite, near Denby, at the time of the 1674 allegations. While most of the prominent families in the area intermarried with others of the locality, it has been suggested that "The Bosvilles were a cut above the rest and chose their marriage partners from much further afield."[143]

Fig. 17. While the Bosville's Gunthwaite Hall no longer exists, its mid-16th century barn is still in use. (Dransfield, 1906)

Colonel Bosville had served as MP for the constituency of Warwick for much of what became known as the Long Parliament, which began in 1640. He led a regiment of foot and it has been claimed that, because he was a large landowner, he was able to recruit over a thousand men to fight on behalf of Cromwell.[144] His commitment to the Parliamentary cause was allied to strong Puritanical religious belief, with Bosville being a chaplain to his soldiers as well as their colonel.[145] Moorhouse noted that, although he never actually sat, he had been appointed to the High Court of Justice in 1648 for the trial of Charles I and was appointed one of the Treasurers at War during the following year. [146] Legislation had been passed in 1649 to enable the raising of £90,000 each month towards the maintenance of the Parliamentary Army and Bosville was one of the 37 named in the Act responsible for levying and distributing the funding.

After his father-in-law's death in 1658, Dransfield suggests that because the third Godfrey Bosville was still a minor, George Sedascue was involved in receiving the Gunthwaite estate rents, along with George Barnby,[147] whose signature is the second on the witchcraft petition. Barnby has been deemed "a zealous friend of the (Bosville)

58

family"[148] but we cannot be absolutely certain that he and the "Mr Barnby" recorded residing in a Denby property with five hearths in 1672[149] were one and the same. However, the likelihood is that the Mr. George Barnby, buried on 24 July, 1683 at Cawthorne, was the petitioner. His status, with the address of "Mr," is recorded in the burial register as it was on the Hearth Tax return.

The extensive Barnby pedigree featuring in Joseph Hunter's "South Yorkshire"[150] contains no use of the first name George but ceases around the time this gentleman is likely have been born. His locative surname seems to place him firmly in the ranks of the family originating from Barnby, near Cawthorne. Prince's history of the nearby parish of Silkstone states that Barnby "...through many centuries was the seat of a family which derived from it their hereditary name and ranked with the principal gentry of these parts of the County."[151] However, a closer look at the history of the Barnby family of Barnby does raise some interesting questions as to whether the petitioner was of the same religious outlook as Sedascue and the Bosvilles. The Spencer-Stanhope archives contain deeds and papers of the Barnby family which clearly evidence that they were of the Catholic faith. Documents relating to their recusancy stretch from 1592 through to well into the 17th century.

A particularly interesting receipt for £10, issued by one of the local Wentworth magistracies to a Thomas Barnby, of Barnby Hall, in 1630, concerns the discharge of a composition for compounding fines for not attending, and receiving a knighthood, at the King's coronation.[152] Presumably this would have related to the enthronement of Charles I, five years earlier. While it is not impossible that the petitioner, George Barnby, retained the family faith, his close association with Sedascue and the Bosvilles raises serious questions as to whether that was actually the case. It is a matter of great regret that the 1676 ecclesiastical census,[153] which gave details of the numbers of Conformists, Papists and Non-conformists locally, had no return for Penistone parish, so even that rough estimate of the different adherents cannot offer any possible insights. Neighbouring Silkstone returned just 1 "Papish recusant" out of a total of 759 inhabitants over 16 years of age. While their return of just 20 of this number who were deemed "Dissenters"[154] is likely to have been an underestimate, from our knowledge of Penistone parish just a couple of years earlier, it is difficult not to feel that their proportion of the population here would have been considerably higher.

The most unique signature on the petition follows immediately behind that of Barnby. Bearing in mind that the Denby witchcraft case concerned, primarily, allegations made by a 16-year-old girl against two older women, it is testimony to the times that just one woman appears to have signed it. The point has already been made that a majority of the local population at the time would have been illiterate and local marriage registers until well into the C19th have marriage partners and their witnesses frequently signing just with their 'marks'. Not many women in the Penistone parish during 1674 would have had the ability to sign their names or the independence of mind to stand up in public support of Hinchliffe and Shillitoe, but Elizabeth Shirt was able and willing to endorse the testimony in their favour.

The Shirt surname may nowadays be quite unusual but in 17th century Cawthorne, not far from where the accused resided, it was relatively common and a John Shirte is noted occupying Dowell Bank there from at least as far back as 1592.[155] The Hearth Tax returns of 1672 record three Shirt households there, two of which had a liability for four hearths, evidencing some wealth. A further Cawthorne entry for a Sherrit – most likely a variant of Shirt – also indicated four hearths.[156] The Spencer Stanhope archives from the mid-17th century feature John Shirt, a "yeoman" and Matthew Shirt, a "gent", both residing in Cawthorne Lanes - what we would now know as North and South Lanes, to the south- west of the village. The prominence of the Shirts at the time is underlined by the fact that another Matthew Shirt, the younger son of John, was studying at St. John's College, Cambridge, during 1662, and likely to have been the

"Matthew Shirte of Fixby, Yks., Clerk", a rector in that Huddersfield parish in 1665.[157]

The Penistone parish registers record the marriage of Ricardus (Richard) Shirt to Elizabeth Kell on 10 August, 1648. Kell is a very unusual surname within the old West Riding of Yorkshire but Kells were recorded in the early C17th records for Darton, the adjacent parish to Cawthorne. Thomas Kell and Anne Webster married at Darton Church on 3 July, 1614 and had several children, including an Elizabeth, who was baptised there on 17 September, 1626. The particular difficulties in establishing individual identity from the patchy surviving records of early modern England are well illustrated by the challenge of determining Elizabeth Shirt's parentage. It was the usual practice then for a bride to marry in her home parish so does the 1648 marriage at Penistone rule out the daughter of the Darton Kells? The Penistone records contain the marriage of Richard Kell to Elizabeth Lee (or Leighe) on 21 April, 1616, and they appear to have had a daughter, Johana, baptised there on 12 December, 1630. They will no doubt have had other children before Johana. Bearing in mind it was common to name the first child of either gender after a parent, was the Elizabeth Kell marrying in 1648 actually a child of Richard and Elizabeth, with the wedding taking place in her own birth parish?

Irrespective of her parentage, it seems certain that the Elizabeth Shirt signing the petition was the "Mrs Ellizabeth Shirt" recorded as a resident of Ingbirchworth in the 1672 Hearth Tax return.[158] She was occupying a substantial four hearth property at the time and her status is indicated by the fact that, although her husband would appear to have been dead by then, she was not entered on the return as "Widow Shirt", in the way most other widowed women were, but accorded the title of "Mrs". Exactly what drew Elizabeth Shirt to support the petition is not clear but the political and religious outlook of quite a number of those who appended their names may well have played a part.

61

Adam Eyre's diaries,[159] from a quarter of a century earlier, strongly feature a fellow Parliamentary army captain by the name of Shirt, residing at the time at Rawroyd, near Cawthorne. Eyre lived at Hazlehead, between Penistone and Holmfirth, but evidently visited Captain Shirt on a quite regular basis, with Shirt also often coming in the other direction. Eyre also mentions his regular contact with a John Shirt of Cawthorne who was steward to Godfrey Bosville when, during the Commonwealth period, as both an MP and army Colonel, he would have spent much time away from Gunthwaite. In his role, Shirt would have overseen Gunthwaite estate affairs. Marrying into the Shirt family at a time when so many of that name were associated with the Parliamentary cause in the Civil War, it might be expected that Elizabeth would share their political and religious outlook.

8. The petition (iii): a race of yeomanry and their minister

The Hearth Tax assessments indicate that, in addition to Elizabeth Shirt's property, there were, in Ingbirchworth at the time, just eleven other occupied houses.[160] But, strikingly, of the dozen individuals and families residing in that small community in 1672, at least four of the heads of household signed the petition two years later. Establishing exactly who they all were is complicated by the fact that several of them share exactly the same first and family names. As well as being certain that Elizabeth Shirt was a signatory, it seems highly likely that the George Firth whose name is also on it, was the Ingbirchworth resident assessed two years earlier as having a two hearth liability. The local Firth connection with early Quakers is the subject of an entire chapter in Bower and Knight's detailed account of their history at Wooldale, High Flatts and Midhope, which focuses, in particular, upon the branch of the family located at Shepley Lane Head[161], close to what is nowadays more commonly known as the Sovereign crossroads, between New Mill and Denby Dale. It seems most likely that this branch were descendants of James Firth who had farmed lands at Lower Cumberworth and Denby Dale from Leak Hall, on the north side of the upper Dearne Valley, from the 16th century.

One account of the history of Denby Dale Parish states that his son, John, born there in 1597, "…became an ardent follower of George Fox, the founder of 'The Society of Friends', and being converted by Fox, he began to hold Quaker meetings in the district."[162] The previously mentioned Christopher Firth, another signatory, may have been a member of this branch but it has not been possible to confirm this.

Determining the identity of the signatory immediately below George Firth – that of George Shaw – is also difficult as there were two of that name, "senior" and "junior", recorded in Ingbirchworth during 1672.[163] Dransfield includes in his Penistone history what he terms "Extracts from Parish Books of Penistone," and it refers to a

1677 memorandum recording an exchange of parish office at the time. It reads "That Widow Roebuck was chosen Churchwarden (for Denby Quarter) and George Shawe Overseer, but that they made an exchange of office by mutual consent."[164] The Hearth Tax returns note a John Roebuck as a near neighbour of both Shaw senior and junior in Ingbirchworth, which is very close to the boundary with Kirkburton parish where the burial of a John Roebuck is recorded on 16 March, 1674. It seems likely that the Shaw who had become the Churchwarden was the signatory and probably the George Shaw, senior, if he was still alive by 1677.

The John Micklethwaite signature on the petition is close to that of George Shaw's but there were three John Micklethwaites listed in Ingbirchworth during 1672. The Hearth Tax returns record one of them as the son of Richard and another as the son of Anthony.[165] This is a very local surname, originating from an ancient farmstead of that name which is now known as Banks, situated within Cawthorne parish, between that village, Silkstone and Hoylandswaine. It is a classic example of a locative family name and George Redmonds has traced its occurrence within the Penistone parish to as far back as c. 1265.[166] He identified its use in Ingbirchworth within the Poll Tax returns of 1379, when a "John de Mekkelhawayth" is listed.[167] A later John Micklethwaite built a – still surviving – house and barn there in 1624.[168]

Joseph Hunter's "South Yorkshire" suggests that "Ing Birchworth...seems never to have been more than a few farms cultivated by a race of yeomanry, and it is only in respect of one point that it affords any materials for topography. In all the parochial proceedings at Peniston we for ever meet the name of Micklethwaite. This was the residence of the family..."[169] But while Hunter's limited Micklethwaite pedigree, featuring several generations of Johns, offers little clarity on the identity of the petitioner, Adam Eyre's frequent contact with the Micklethwaites perhaps narrows it down a little.

Fig. 18. **Micklethwaite House, Ingbirchworth.**
(Courtesy of Penistone History Archive)

The Hearth Tax returns of 1672 note the existence of a forge at Ingbirchworth, operated then by a William Barker[170] and, some years earlier, by someone called Thorp who Eyre paid to shoe his horse. When he visited Thorp's smithy, it seems to have been his practice to call in on a John Micklethwaite and Eyre appears to distinguish him from another Micklethwaite – possibly his father – to whom he refers as "Old John"[171]

In terms of where these various Johns lived, while the location of the son of Anthony Micklethwaite is unclear, from Eyre's records[172] there is some suggestion that the son of Richard may have lived at what is now known as Annat Royd, to the south of the present day Ingbirchworth reservoir. The John Micklethwaite with whom Adam Eyre interacted most was involved with him in the extensive endeavours to remove Christopher Dickinson as Penistone vicar and it seems that this Micklethwaite was the representative of the local township on this matter within the wider Penistone parish. At the time, it was common in such large parishes for these townships to take on responsibility for highway maintenance and the administration of the local Poor Law. As Eyre bought wheat from him,[173] Micklethwaite would appear to have been an arable farmer of some substance, occupying a five hearth property in 1672, which Eyre earlier terms Overhouse.[174] Eyre's diary has several references to the terminal illness of John's wife, Dyonis, during 1647, and the fact that it prevented him taking one of their unmarried daughters as a maid.[175] With daughters probably in their teens at this time, it is highly likely that Dyonis's widower was still alive in 1674 and supported the petition.

Micklethwaite's leading role within the local township would have meant his regular contact with other key local figures whose names also appear on the petition. He would have known well the Rev. Timothy Kent, who served as the minister at Denby Church from 1665 until his death in 1691. The second Act of Uniformity, passed in 1552, as well as requiring the use of the second Book of Common Prayer, had imposed fines for failing to attend services at the local parish church. For those nearing the northern boundaries of Penistone parish, travelling to Penistone Church on foot, in carts or on horseback could be a difficult journey in bad weather. In the years before the building of a bridge over Scout Stream and the construction of the Scout Dike reservoir during the 1920s, crossing at its ford was particularly challenging in times of flood. It was the tragic loss of the lives of thirteen parishioners crossing the stream during 1626 that led to the establishment of the Denby Chapel as a chapel-of-ease and its consecration by the Archbishop of York during the following year.

Dransfield remarked that "The foundation of this chapel...is to be attributed to the spirit of puritanism which grew strong in the reign of James I and Charles I."[176] He credits the second Godfrey Bosville of Gunthwaite with establishing the tradition of puritan ministers[177] but his account of their identities offers little information on Timothy Kent, beyond very basic detail from his epitaph inside the chapel.

Fig. 19. Denby Church, originally a chapel-of-ease within Penistone parish, opened in 1627. (D. Hinchliffe)

Bearing in mind that he was at Denby for over a quarter of a century this is quite surprising, but there are few other clues to his background and the Hearth Tax returns for 1672 have no-one of that name listed within the Denby township or the wider Penistone parish. Just one person named Timothy Kent appears in the returns for the whole of the old West Riding, living in a substantial property some fifteen miles to the north, in Briggate, Leeds.[178]

It is possible, but unlikely, that the Denby minister was a member of what seems to have been quite a wealthy Leeds family, apparently associated with some of the early industrialists of the city towards the end of the previous century.[179] An alternative – perhaps more

67

credible – lineage is that of the wider Kent family who feature in Lincolnshire during the earlier years of the C17th because, from the very limited available records, there does appear to be some tradition of priesthood, like that of the Oleys. It may be entirely coincidental, but the parish church of St. Martin in Withcall, Lincolnshire, had a Timothy Kent as its rector from 1622 until his death in 1624 when he was succeeded by a Thomas Kent, whose death is recorded in 1638.[180]

9. The petition (iv): Burdett backing

What is likely to have been one of the old routes from Gunthwaite, in the direction of Penistone, heads west from Gunthwaite Hall then south over Clough Dike, nowadays crossing the Huddersfield to Sheffield rail line and joining Carr Head Lane not far from where Elizabeth Shirt lived in Ingbirchworth. This short lane leads from what is now the A629 Huddersfield Road to Carr Head, a property being farmed during the early years of the C17th by a Richard Burdett, who was noted in a tithing document of 1617 as a "gentleman".[181] His wife, Barbary, survived him and is described as his widow in June, 1656.[182] The property appears held by their daughter and heir, Mary, by 1640,[183] prior to her marriage into the Shaw family of Newhouse,[184] and it is one of a number of important local properties to which the Burdetts were connected during the years preceding the Denby witchcraft allegation.

Five different Burdett signatures can be identified on the petition, the most for one individual family name, and their support strongly underlines how, at its core, was a similar religious outlook. David Hey describes the Burdetts as among the families who "... were Puritans before and during the Commonwealth and staunch Non-Conformists in later times."[185] But as, arguably, Denby's most long established family, the Burdett name carried great weight and influence. Joseph Hunter has suggested that their connection with it began during the reign of Edward I (1272-1307) when Robert Burdet married Idonea, the Lady of Denby, and daughter and heir of Robert de Balliol.[186] Their son, Aymer, was the first in many generations to be recorded with that Christian name and the Spencer-Stanhope archives record an Ailmer Burdett occupying Denby Hall, to the east of Lower Denby, during the 1570s.[187]

Aymer and Ailmer had numerous variant spellings, including Aylmer, Adomar, Amore and, perhaps the most used, Amer.[188] But, among the Burdett signatures which can be ascertained is one where the Christian name appears to be Emoria, another spelling derived from whatever the original may have been. It is most likely to have been that of Emor Burdett who was taxed in Denby in 1672 on the basis of having three hearths and George Redmonds has noted that, during that same year, he appears to have been party to a dispute with the prominent Beaumont family of Whitley, to the west of Thornhill, near Dewsbury.[189]

Emoria Burdett's signature follows that of Thomas Burditt who appears to be the occupant of a substantial five hearth property, similarly in Denby, during 1672.[190] That name also features six years on from the witchcraft case, with a Thomas Burdet of Denby listed in Sir Michael Wentworth's militia during 1680.[191] George Burditt, whose signature features just below Emoria's on the petition, appears in the Hearth Tax return with a liability for a more modest two hearth property in Denby and has the same variant of the surname as Thomas. Tobias Burdett is the last of the Burdetts resident in Denby, recorded in 1672 as having a substantial four hearth house. [192]The final Burdett signature would appear to be that of Sir Francis Burdett who was resident further afield in Kexbrough, to the north of Cawthorne, at the time of the Hearth Tax and occupying Birthwaite (or Burthwaite) Hall, a sizeable property.

Unravelling the origins and connections of these individual Burdetts is challenging but Joseph Hunter has suggested that "Richard Burdet, in the reign of Henry VIII, weakened the family by dividing it into two principal branches," one of which lived at Birthwaite Hall.[193] A dispute with his eldest son, Aymor, had led to Richard splitting his estate, which included the manors of Denby and (High) Hoyland between Aymor and his brother, Thomas. Hunter notes the size of the estate which had "…17 messuages (dwelling houses with surrounding property), 1200 acres of land, 500 of meadow, 4000 of pasture, 1200 of wood, a water-mill, two fulling mills…", as well as £9.10s rental income.[194]

The (High) Hoyland manor would have included Birthwaite Hall where Sir Francis is likely to have been living at the time of the petition and the possible historical disconnect within the Burdetts, mentioned by Hunter, might account for the fact that his signature is appended a considerable distance from the others of the same surname or variants on the petition. Alternatively, as has previously been suggested, the order in which the signatures appear may simply reflect its progress around the local area.

10. The petition (v): Cat Hill and Hoylandswaine

Oliver Heywood's familiarity with a number of the petitioners suggests that they are likely to have also closely adhered at the time to his non-conformist faith. He travelled remarkable distances, usually on horseback, preaching in various parts of the north and often visiting followers, frequently staying with them as he moved around. His contacts within the Penistone parish around the time of the witchcraft case are further evidence of a common theological thread among those who supported Hinchliffe and Shillitoe.

One likely route between Lower Denby, Denby Hall and the parish church in Penistone at the time would have been south, alongside Broad Oak, passing Gunthwaite dam and mill and heading up the steep hill now known as Cat Hill Lane. Prince's history of Silkstone suggests that what was originally known as Catling Hall, in the township of Hoylandswaine, "...derived its name from a family so called, who appear in early charters."[195] There had been Catlyns in the Penistone area from at least 1441 and a Catlen is noted within the parish in the mid-C16th.[196]

Fig. 20. Cat Hill Hall, in Hoylandswaine township.
(Courtesy of Penistone History Archive).

The Spencer-Stanhope archives contain numerous documents relating to the Sotwell family in that locality, with one within their deeds and papers appearing to show the sale of Cathill to "Margaret

Setwell, of Penistone, Spinster" on 20 July, 1587[197] and it has been recorded that a John Sotwell served as vicar of Penistone from 1574 to 1597, being originally 'presented' by "Godfrey Bosvill".[198]Later C18th documents contained in the archives refer to an "Elizabeth Sitwell"[199] and it is open to debate whether what appear to be variants of Sotwell originated with the surname Suthwell or Southwell, recorded in York as far back as 1394.[200]

Heywood's contact in Cat Hill is with the Sotwells and his diary has various entries of visits there from November, 1666, through to the Autumn of the year the witchcraft allegations were made, eight years later.[201] Cat Hill Hall, or Manor, was clearly a substantial property, liable for a Hearth Tax contribution for 8 hearths in 1672 when a "Mr John Setwell" was recorded as the occupant.[202] He is likely to have been the "Jo Sotwell" who signed the witchcraft petition and was evidently a religious adherent of Heywood. The diary entries relating to his Cat Hill visits raise the question as to whether the travelling preacher might have had any direct role in the enlistment of some of the petitioners, as he obviously knew a number of them very well.

Heywood recorded staying at Cat Hill and his subsequent contact with these petitioners while he was in the area. A number of his visits around 1666/7 may have been motivated by a concern over the longstanding serious illness of Sotwell's wife. His diary for 10 December, 1666, records "On the Munday I visited Mtris. Sotwell of Cat-hil in Silkstone parish, being sick, and dined at gunthwaite with Major Sedascue a german."[203] He seems to have used Cat Hill as a form of retreat and records on 1 July, 1670, "...on Friday to Mr. Sotwells of Cat-Hill, stayed there studying till lords day morning, thence went to Peniston, preacht all day quietly in the church where there was a numerous congregation."[204] Heywood's diary records his being pursued for his beliefs and the relative seclusion of Cat Hill may have offered him a degree of security. The few houses on that hill do seem to have played a key role in local nonconformity around this time. Living close to Cat Hill Hall, Joseph Clark had 10 years earlier, in 1660, been jailed for three weeks for being at a Quaker meeting.[205]

The Thomas Walshaw signing the petition is noted as a resident of Hoylandswaine within the 1672 Hearth Tax returns but appears to have had a connection to nearby Carr Head, which has already been mentioned, from two decades earlier. The Spencer-Stanhope archives note the sale of "Carhead" to "John Sotwell of Cathill and Thomas Wallshaw of Horbery, Yeoman" on 5 October, 1652.[207] A later 'deed of partition' records an agreement over the apportionment of lands between "John Sotwell of Cathill, Gent, and Thomas Walshawe of Carhead, Yeoman" on 29 March, 1656.[208] Walshaw's entry in the 1672 returns denotes his occupation of a three-hearth property. A particularly difficult to identify signature on the petition is likely to have been that of John Wallom, occupying a similar size house in the area close to Sotwell and Walshaw.

Nor far to the east of Cat Hill is located Hoyland Swaine which is recorded in the 1674 Hearth Tax as the home of Christopher Green[209], and a "Christopher Greene" also signed the petition. It has not been possible to confirm this, but his residence here suggests a likely family connection with the yeoman Green family who occupied Micklethwaite (later Banks) and Elmhirst,[210] both to the south west of Cawthorne, and close to South Lane, leading to Hoyland Swaine, during the 17th century.

74

11. The petition (vi): more Penistone people

Another entry in Heywood's diary notes John Sotwell's association with the next signatory to him on the petition, Sylvanus Rich. The Riches occupied several properties in the Penistone area during the C17th, most notably Bullhouse Hall, to the west of Thurlstone and Millhouse Green. Various members of the family feature prominently in the diary of Adam Eyre of Hazlehead, between Penistone and Holmfirth, the Parliamentary Army captain during the Civil Wars.[211] Eyre had a very close personal relationship with fellow Parliamentary Captain, William Rich, who served under Lord Fairfax, and Sylvanus was his son and heir.

Fig. 22. Bullhouse Hall. (Dransfield, 1906)

William Rich gave his son a biblical name favoured in Puritan circles and Sylvanus subsequently demonstrated his own religious commitment by initiating worship at Bullhouse prior to the later establishment of the Bullhouse Chapel. In the early years following the restoration of the monarchy in 1660 there had been considerable national focus on action to prevent the Puritans returning to power. Legislation was passed compelling the use of a revised Church of England prayer book, with the end result that Puritan ministers, such as Staniforth, who drew up the petition, were driven from the livings they had held during the Commonwealth period. He was by no means alone at the time as around one in five clergy with a similar outlook were also ejected. As Richards has put it, "Henceforward the best the Puritans could strive for was not control within the Church, but toleration outside the Church."[212]

Two years before the witchcraft case, Charles II introduced a measure allowing Catholics to conduct worship in their own houses and non-conformists to worship in public. Sylvanus Rich acted on these new permissions by obtaining a license to allow his home at Bullhouse Hall to be used for religious meetings. But if his character might be assumed to have been rooted in a rigid Puritanical form of non-conformity, Oliver Heywood's record from the time might question this. He noted that during the autumn of 1674, not long after the witchcraft claims had been made, Rich had been at Wakefield Fair with John Sotwell and others from the Penistone area. After "...having drunk too liberally...",[213] heading home in the dark, Rich and his horse found themselves in the swollen River Calder. He eventually grabbed a tree branch, hauled himself out and caught up with the horse which had also extracted itself from the water. Heywood describes Rich's experience as "...a miraculous providence and fair warning! I pray God it may awaken conscience, this man hath made a profession, entertained ministers and meetings at this house, but of late hath given over, often stays out late, comes home in the night, ventures through dangerous waters, Lord strike home by this providence."[214]

Sylvanus Rich was linked, through marriage, to another prominent Penistone family, the Wordsworths, who were also involved in supporting the petition. He married Mary, the daughter of Ralph Wordsworth, of Water Hall, at Sheffield on 22 April, 1652. Water Hall, to the north of Penistone, is close to what was, at that time, known as Denby Bridge, but is now called Bridge End. Ralph had been one of the Lords of the Manor of Penistone and, also, Chief Constable of the Staincross wapentake during 1648.[215] Around the same time, he was serving as churchwarden at Penistone and he featured quite regularly – often as a creditor – in Captain Adam Eyre's diaries.[216] He was succeeded, on his death in 1663, by his second son, Josias, and the will of Eyre's wife, Susannah, in 1668, indicates a continuing indebtedness, bequeathing to him "...my great pann, for and towards the satisfaction and payment of a certaine sume of money which I have appointed him to pay to the executors of Ralph Wordsworth, his father."

Fig. 23. Water Hall, Penistone. (Dransfield, 1906)

The Wordsworths had longstanding roots in and around Penistone, with a "Nicholas Wurdesworth" witnessing a deed in the area as far back as 1392.[217] Josias appears to be one of the two Wordsworth signatures in 1674, with Ambrose the other. Both feature as "Wadsworth" in the Penistone Hearth Tax returns, with Josias liable for seven hearths at Water Hall and Ambrose having a more modest property, with just four,[218] at Schole Hill, between Penistone and

Cubley. As one of several attorneys appointed to act on behalf of William Wordsworth of Falthwaite, in 1666, Ambrose is described as "gent"[219] and it is not clear if his self-description as "yeoman" in his will dated 9 September, 1675,[220] indicates any decline in his fortunes during that preceding decade. The author of the witchcraft petition, Nathan Staniforth, was one of the witnesses to the will.

Staniforth, of course, appended his name to numerous official documents in Penistone parish around this time but his written presence in the local history of the area is perhaps minimal in comparison to that of the Wordworths over very many years. As John Dransfield remarked, from the reign of Edward III, "...no name appears more frequently as witnesses or principals in deeds relating to this parish, or in connection with parochial affairs."[221]

12. The petition (vii): religious dissidents

The signature immediately preceding Josias Wordsworth on the petition appears to be that of William Cotton who, by 1674, was living at Denby Hall. His non-conformist sympathies are apparent from Oliver Heywood's extensive records of contact with him between 1666 and 1670 when he was living at "Moore End", near Silkstone.[222]

The purchase of what is now known as Dodworth Moor End took place in 1656, with Cotton then being described as of "Wortley Forge".[223] When John Spofford, the 74 year old Vicar of Silkstone was ejected from his living for refusing to abide by the Act of Uniformity, he was taken in by the longstanding ironmaster.[224] Heywood records on 2 March, 1667/8 "...On Munday I travelled to visit old Mr. Spawford at Mr. Cotton's house..."[225] The diaries evidence that Cotton was at still at Moor End in July, 1670,[226] but, by April, 1672, notes "We kept a fast at Mr. Cotton's at Denbigh – had a considerable company." [227] The fact Cotton had not resided at Denby for very long at the time of the witchcraft allegations is confirmed by the qualification alongside his signature on the petition supporting the accused, which reads "from the time of his knowledge of them".

Denby Hall, under William Cotton, would have featured such religious observation as, like Sylvanus Rich's home at Bullhouse, it was licensed as a meeting place for non-conformists under the 1672 legislation. The exact nature of their worship is a matter of debate but David Hey has suggested that, along with members of the Burdett, Rich and Wordsworth families, the Cottons became Quakers.[228] Signing the petition could well have been one of the last formal acts of his life as Dransfield records the burial of "William Cotton of Nether Denby, Gent.," in 1674.[229] In his 'Event Book', Oliver Heywood has a section headed "Useful men in a private capacity dead of late". He includes the fact that "Mr Willm Cotton was buryed at Peniston March 17 1674/5. We were 8 non-conformist ministers at his funeral, great lamentation."[230]

Cotton's support for Henry Swift, the Puritan vicar of Penistone, has been credited with contributing to him retaining his living[231] during a time when his religious practice had, by 1672, led to him being imprisoned for some three months at one point, according to Heywood.[232] Swift had been in post for some forty years when he died suddenly in 1689, aged 66,[233]so he would have been the Penistone incumbent at the time of the witchcraft case. While it is not possible to make out his signature on the petition, there are at least three other signatories on it who appear to share his surname.

Swifts feature in local records at least from as far back as 1528 when two John Swifts – senior and junior – are recorded in Silkstone.[234] From the late 16th century, several generations appear in documents relating to Nabbs or Nabbes and later Nabbs Hall, together with Silkstone Fall and its smithies.[235]During the first quarter of the C17th, a William Swifte is mentioned in a tithing document relating to Hoylandswaine[236] and his description as "Clerk" suggests the possibility of a longstanding religious commitment among some of this name within the Penistone area. Adam Eyre mentioned in his diaries that, during March, 1646/7, a "Ra. Swift" and a "Jo. Swift" were both signatories on a petition calling for the removal of Henry Swift's predecessor as Penistone incumbent, Christopher Dickinson, amid allegations concerning his Civil War sympathies, the manner of his 'appointment', his preaching limitations, drunkenness and having kept "base lewd company".[237]

The Ralph Swift featuring in the later 1674 petition is likely to have been the resident of Denby noted in the Hearth Tax returns two years earlier to have been occupying a two hearth property.[238] The identity of the signatory, Joseph Swift is less clear, as the only person of that name locally is resident in Shafton, some distance to the east – between Royston and Hemsworth – in 1672.[239] The John Swift on it would have been the occupant of another two-hearth property at Gunthwaite recorded in the same returns.[240] Bearing in mind that the Cottons of Denby apparently became Quakers, it seems that yet another of the petitioners converted as well, because Bower and

Knight, in their history of the Quakers of Wooldale, High Flatts and Midhope, state that John Swift of Gunthwaite was among "A large number of early local Friends..."[241]

Just below Ralph Swift's signature on the petition is that of another local man who would seem to have played an important role in the establishment of the High Flatts Friends Meeting House. The person listed as "Joseph Baley" – like Swift, living in a two hearth Denby property in 1672[242] - appears to have signed his name as "Joseph Bayley". It has already been noted that the reference to Quaker Hall dike in one of the Moor depositions may have related to the use, by 1674, of a barn at High Flatts for worship. High Flatts was within Denby township in 1672 and Bayley's tax liability could have related to a residence within what is now the hamlet in which the Meeting House is located.

With very limited information available from the parish records of the time and the frequent practice of naming a first son after his father, there is always the chance that the Joseph Bayley in the petition was of the previous generation to the person of the same name credited with handing over premises at High Flatts to the Friends' trustees in 1701.[243] It is still to this day possible to see a date stone from 1697 on the north wall of the Meeting House which contains the initials "J.E.B.", believed to be those of Joseph Bayley and his wife Elizabeth.[244] Whilst accepting it is conceivable the petitioner could have been this Joseph's father, the strong likelihood is that he was this key figure in the early days of worship at High Flatts. It seems yet another strong link between the petitioners and the early Quaker faith.

A similar connection seems likely in the case of John Couldwell, whose name is another on the petition. This signature is likely to be that of the "John Cordwell" of Thurlstone, noted in the 1672 Hearth Tax returns as occupying a two hearth property.[245] This man was probably a member of the longstanding Couldwell family of Thurlstone.

Fig. 24. Date stone on Quaker Meeting House, High Flatts.(D. Hinchliffe)

It has been suggested that Judd Field Farm, to the south of Penistone, was used as a Quaker meeting place when occupied by the Couldwells.[246]A John Couldwell is among a group of local Friends who faced trial in 1683 for failing to attend Penistone Church, when one of the Wordsworths was similarly charged.[247]

The John Jessop signature will have been that of the Penistone resident of that name who was probably related to the Thomas Jessop of Denby who also appears to have supported Hinchliffe and Shillitoe. George Redmonds has identified a Thomas Jessop who was a Denby stone-mason as being among over forty men summoned before the courts in 1666 accused of participating in "an act of religious adoration, contrary to the law." The congregation of Jessop and his co-accused was described as "...a riot, or unlawful assembly, which had put the local population in great fear."[248]

Another Thurlstone signatory was Nicholas Saunderson, who appears as "Nichollas Sanderson" in the Hearth Tax returns.[249] His one hearth liability gives the impression he was of humble stock but his name is shared with that of one of Penistone's most famous sons, the blind boy who ended up as the Lucasian Professor of

Mathematics at Cambridge University. He was born in Thurlstone in 1682, to John and Anne Saunderson, and is likely to have been named after his paternal grandfather, the petitioner. Having lost his sight during his second year of life, young Nicholas later attended Penistone Grammar School under the tutelage of the petition's author, Nathan Staniforth, and from him it is suggested "...he acquired no inconsiderable classical and mathematical knowledge."[250]

13. The petition (viii): Gaunts… and Papists?

Three signatories with the surname Gaunt appear on the petition but information concerning the backgrounds of Robert, Thomas and William is difficult to come by. The "de Gaunt" surname is recorded in Holmfirth as far back as 1308[251] but its occurrence within the Penistone parish is minimal. Hoylandswaine belonged to the adjacent Silkstone parish in 1618 when there is mention of a "Thomas Gawnt" in respect of tithe collection in the area[252] and it is open to question whether the Thomas Gaunt marrying Susanna Warde at Penistone during 1667 is a descendent and the petitioner. It is more certain that he is the Denby resident in 1672 in the Hearth Tax return with a two hearth property and that the William Gaunt supporting the accused women is the one recorded, also in Denby, with just one hearth.[253] It is conceivable that a Robert Gaunt had moved into the parish between 1672 and 1674 but the only Robert Gaunt recorded in the Hearth Tax return for the whole of the West Riding is some way to the east, in Tickhill, south of Doncaster.[254]

If a broad consensus in terms of religious outlook appears to be a common theme among the petitioners, the signature of Robert Blackburn might possibly suggest that concerns over the accusations were shared well beyond those adhering to Oliver Heywood's beliefs. The Blackburns were a prominent Roman Catholic family with connections to various properties and land within the Penistone parish, including at Cotes (or Coates) in Thurgoland[255], Hunshelf Hall and Alderman's Head. The listing of a "Robert Blackburne" in a 4 hearth property within the Langsett township in the 1672 Hearth Tax returns suggests that he was probably resident at the latter property at this time but the recurrent use of the same first name for the first-born son over a number of generations of the family makes confirming him as the signatory a little difficult. This Robert could have been living much closer to Hinchliffe and Shillitoe at the time of the case, as one substantial property there passed down through several generations of the Blackburns. Dransfield wrote of "The old house at Denby named in the maps as Papist Hall, which is only a name of vulgar reproach given to it by the people around, is a favourable specimen of the houses of the better sort of yeomanry in the time of Charles II. It belonged to the family of Blackburn, who were Catholics."[256]

Papist Hall is located at the junction of Denby Lane and Lower Denby Lane in Lower Denby. It nowadays consists of a sizeable house, which dates from the Victorian period, and two rather older large barns. The one to the north has two date stones, one of which appears to be from 1632 and has on it the name of a "Robart Blackeburn." It is unlikely that he was the same person, but a Robert Blackburn was known to have been a trustee of Penistone Grammar School at the time of the witchcraft case[257] and his connection to the petition may have come as a result of his contact with the likes of Nathan Staniforth, the School's clerk. In addition, the land held by the Blackburns at Cotes, in Thurgoland, was very close to the Wortley Top Forge which had been operated by another prominent petitioner, William Cotton.

Left: Fig. 25. The date stones on the north barn at Papist Hall, Lower Denby.
(D. Hinchliffe)

The Penistone parish records record the marriage of "Robert Blackburne" to Elizabeth Greaves on 13 May, 1658, and the Greaves surname features just a little below that of Blackburn on the petition. The signature is that of Thomas Greaves who is also mentioned by Dransfield as having been a Grammar School trustee, serving alongside fellow petitioners Josias and Ambrose Wordsworth.[258] Adam Eyre's diaries make mention of various members of the Greaves family who are living not far from his home in Hazlehead, at Smallshaw, Catshaw and Shephouse. In 1672 he is listed in the Penistone Hearth Tax returns immediately below the vicar, Henry Swift, and the two Wordsworths, occupying a substantial 5 hearth property.[259]

Another petitioner with connections to Penistone Grammar School was William Beever who was occupying a similarly sizeable property in Thurlstone during 1672. This surname appears under several variants in 17th century records in the area and Dransfield refers to a "William Beevor, Yeo." being a trustee of the School in 1677.[260] A memorial in Penistone Church marks the death of "William Beevor of Thurlston, Dyer" during 1684, aged 58. Along with Beever, another Thurlstone signatory was Ralph Marsden.

Thurlstone has the only two entries in the entire West Riding Hearth Tax returns for the family name Outheram[261] and this surname (or a variant) featured in Upper Denby over a century later. The cottage, known as Marshall House, has, over its entrance, a datestone of 1770 and initials which are believed to be those of James and Elizabeth Outeram. It understood to be on the site of an earlier house with the same name and is close to a yard which had been known as Marshall Fold. Two Marshall signatories appear on the 1674 petition, Thomas and Richard. They are likely to be the "Thomas Marshall jun" and "Richard Marshall sen," listed as occupying, respectively, a three hearth and a two hearth property in Denby during 1672.[262] Another Richard Marshall is recorded as living in Thurlstone that year[263] and he is probably the father of the Thomas

Marshall whose baptism is recorded taking place at Penistone Church on 11 March, 1675.

Bearing in mind that the same Christian names are being used, it is highly likely that these men were from the same family and the Marshall surname features in the Denby area from at least the C16th, when a William Marshall is recorded there.[264] Hey notes that, as far back as 1529, "...William Marshall, a Denby yeoman, left a bequest to the chantry priest..."[265] The record of the involvement of a John Marshall of High Hoyland in a Penistone parish tithing dispute towards the end of the C16th[266] might offer a clue as to why Clayton Mill at Scissett, located alongside the old road from High Hoyland to Skelmanthorpe, was previously known as Marshall Mill.[267] His occupation is listed as "Milner" (corn miller). A later C18th family occupation is identified in the will of Elizabeth, the widow of "John Marshall, late of Nether Denby," who was a tanner.[268]

Very close to Marshall House in Upper Denby is Manor Farm, off Bank Lane, another property dating from the late C17th. Manor Farm cottage has a date stone of 1677, with the name of Joseph Mosley indicating he was responsible for its construction, probably – like Marshall House – on the site of a previous property. Joseph Mosley signed the petition and is likely to have been the "Joseph Masley" recorded occupying a three-hearth property in Denby in 1672.[269] The Mosley (or Moseley) surname occurred in West Bretton as far back as 1323 and nearby Cawthorne in 1379.[270] A John Mosley, was farming at Upper Norcroft, between Cawthorne and Silkstone, until the mid-C17th, and an inventory of this property dated 1650, probably following his death, gives a detailed insight into the domestic circumstances of the local yeoman class at the time.[271] It is likely that Joseph was John's son as there is a 1651 record of a "John Mosley of Norcroft, yeoman" leaving Joseph his "messuages" (dwelling house and surrounding property) in Upper Denby.[272] The fact that Denby Delf, the nature reserve to the north of Denby Lane, was traditionally known as Mosley Roughs suggests that the Mosleys may well have had landholdings in the area as well. Joseph Mosley's occupation on the 1651 document is also given as "tanner"[273] and, while this may be coincidental, it has been noted that the overgrown remains of an old tannery can be seen quite close to the former Mosley Roughs where the path from there crosses Munchcliffe Beck, close to the High Flatts Quaker settlement.[274]

Fig. 26. Date stone on Manor Farm Cottage, Upper Denby. (D. Hinchliffe)

If the Hearth Tax returns can be assumed to offer some limited insight into the comparative prosperity of the signatories, then Denby's Richard Hawksworth, with five hearths, features as joint third in the township's wealth stakes. References to the various branches of the Hawksworths in the immediate area are numerous within the Spencer-Stanhope archives, with connections to Wheatley Hill Farm – between Clayton West and Denby – noted in 1588.[275] Adam Eyre's diary records that on 27 March, 1647/8, he was owed money by "Peter Hawkworth of Wheatley hill"[276] and he records frequent contact with a Richard Hawksworth of Denby in relation to efforts to secure the removal of the Penistone incumbent. This Hawksworth is noted by Eyre as being among the churchwardens at Penistone in 1648.[277]

A record from January, 1558/9, notes a yeoman named "William Hawkesworth of Gunthwaite"[278] but this may actually relate to Broad Oak, close to the old Gunthwaite Mill, where a "Peter Hawskworth" was farming a century later in 1661.[279] Dransfield's History of Penistone mentions the burial of 25 year old Dorothy, the wife of Richard Hawksworth of Broad Oak, evidencing that they were still there at the time of her death in 1709.[280]The Hawksworths occur among Denby yeomanry back in 1600 when an earlier Richard Hawksworth is recorded purchasing from the Barnby family a "Toft and tenement called Holdroughlay alias Holdrewlaye, and now called Rowlayes in Cawthorne."[281] Of course, this is the same land near to Jowett House, Cawthorne, which, as has been noted, seems to have later been connected to the Olay family and the Shillitoes.

There is minimal information about several of the remaining signatories but the Richard Shaw `whose name is on it would appear to have been residing within the Gunthwaite township at the time of the Hearth Tax. The John Clayton signatory seems to have been occupying a three-hearth property in Denby two years earlier. While the petition quite clearly was supported by some of the most influential figures within and near to the Penistone parish, the signatures of some - whom the Hearth Tax returns would seem to suggest were by no means wealthy – evidences a possibly greater level of literacy among the less well-off that might have been expected. Immediately underneath the signatures of Thomas, Emoria and George Burdett on it is the signature of Denby's Joseph Pollard, the occupant of a one-hearth property. Richard Prest and John Shaw, having similar humble properties in the same township, seem also to have added their names.

14. A melancholy conclusion

It has the appearance of just another day in Oliver Heywood's 'Event Book'. Tucked away, almost at its end, the penultimate paragraph summarises this story and how it was to end.

One Joseph Hinchlive and his wife being accused of witchcraft, and upon depositions on oath being bound to the assizes, he could not bear it but fainted, went out one Thursday morning Feb 4 1674-5 hanged himself in a wood near his house, was not found till the Lords day, his wife dyed in her bed, spoke and acted as a Christian praying for her adverserys that falsely accused her, was buryed on Feb 4 – before he was found, - I hope she was a good woman - [282]

Perhaps some context should be added to what appears to be the briefest of mentions of what would have been an appalling tragedy. Heywood's diaries and 'Event Book' record the circumstances he came across as a minister and are full of numerous tales of illness, accidents and deaths. He would, of course, be regularly called in to pray for the dying and, during his travels, pick up news of all sorts of adversity which seemed, from his records, to be more or less the day-to-day norm. While he mentions the outcome of the Denby case, it is unlikely that – for him – it ranked as anything especially remarkable.

But from his information – concise as it may be – we are advised of the key detail of the circumstances of how this matter came to a close and precisely when. We are told by Heywood that Joseph Hinchliffe had "fainted" when the case was bound over to the Assizes. His account suggests that it was Hinchliffe and his wife who were to appear at this higher court but the surviving Assize documentation makes it clear that it was actually his wife and daughter who were to face trial. We know that this binding over by Wentworth had occurred during the late summer and early autumn of 1674, with the case likely to be heard at the spring Assizes of 1674/5. Joseph and Susanna Hinchliffe and Anne Shillitoe would have had these allegations hanging over them throughout the autumn and winter, in the full knowledge that a death sentence was a distinct possibility for the two women. The fact that a petition, signed by some of the most distinguished individuals in their area, had made absolutely no difference to the case being referred to the Assizes will have added to their fears that the very worst possible outcome was highly likely. An added possibility arises from Heywood's understanding that it was just Joseph and Susanna who were bound over to the Assizes. Bearing in mind that Joseph was clearly implicated by Mary Moor's allegations of what she had heard said about his 'powers', were there subsequent charges laid that involved him and not his daughter? Heywood's sources will no doubt have been his petitioner contacts within Denby, the wider Penistone parish and elsewhere, and it is questionable how reliable these would be on a matter which had bitterly divided local opinion.   There appears to be no Assize documentation to substantiate the possibility of Joseph having been charged, so we are left with this as just a hypothesis.

Heywood gives us the exact date of when Joseph Hinchliffe hanged himself - Thursday, 4 February, 1674/5 – and we are told this was in a wood near his house. If we are correct in believing this is likely to have been in Lower Denby, his options were several, although the wooded areas back then would not have been what remain today. Obviously, the modern A635 Shepley Lane Head road was many years from its construction, but even before its advent, the area now known as Munchcliffe Woods, which has been previously mentioned, was less than a mile away and easily reached from Lower Denby.

Joseph died shortly before the arrival of the judges on the Northern Circuit for the spring Assize hearings. He would have known the likely date of a court appearance in York and this may well have been a factor in his decision to commit suicide. The implication in the wording of the petition the previous summer was that his wife may not have been in good health and this might also have played a part in his thinking. But the fact that, according to Heywood's account, she was buried on the same day he disappeared would seem to suggest she was most likely dead before he came to the decision to kill himself. At that point, conceivably, he may then have been the only remaining defendant facing the charges.

An alternative possibility, put to me by others with an interest in this case, is that Susanna did not die of natural causes but was murdered by Joseph, who would then flee the scene to take his own life. The suggestion is that this would have been a 'mercy' killing to ensure his wife avoided what, by then, would have seemed her inevitable fate at the conclusion of the Spring Assizes. But, even from just Oliver Heywood's brief account of Susanna's final hours, I believe this to be a most unlikely scenario. Despite the limited sources of information relating to the events of 1674/5, the closeness of the local communities at the time and their clear awareness and concern over the allegations, there is no hint whatsoever of this being the conclusion. The impression we gain of Susanna as a woman of faith perhaps suggests that her husband, too, may have lived his life in strict accordance with Christian principles.

It has not been possible to find any burial record for either Susanna or Joseph. The forthcoming Assize hearing of the case would have been well known and would have possibly complicated the burial arrangements for Susanna on that winter Thursday. Certainly, in some other parishes not too far away, the idea of offering a Christian burial to a woman who had faced what, at the time, were the most serious of allegations, would have definitely not been entertained. But, in Denby, the incumbent at the time, Timothy Kent, was no agnostic on Moor's detailed claims. He had put his name to the strongest possible case for Hinchliffe's complete innocence by signing the petition of support for her and her daughter. If the question of her right to a burial in consecrated ground in Upper Denby was solely a matter for him, there is little doubt as to what would have been his response. And while Rev. Henry Swift, at Penistone Church, does not appear to have been alongside the - at least - three other Swift signatories on the petition, given his religious outlook, the likelihood is that, if a burial at Penistone was proposed

92

and, in mid-winter, feasible, his attitude may have differed little from Kent.

But perhaps, when her husband was found on the following Sunday, 7 February, the arrangements for his burial may not have been quite so straightforward. Heywood's account is categoric in relation to him having taken his own life and the news about the nature of his death by hanging would have quickly spread way beyond the immediate neighbourhood. It would be of some comfort to be able to believe that Kent or Swift would, perhaps, have been able to arrange for Joseph Hinchliffe to be interred alongside Susanna but there was little likelihood of this happening. The ecclesiastical courts of the time required suicide burials to take place on what was deemed "the Devil's side" of the church, to its north, in unconsecrated ground alongside the graves of the unbaptized and excommunicants. Perhaps this was preferable to the alternative of the deceased being buried at a crossroads with steps being taken to destroy evil spirits by a stake driven through their heart.

Exactly where the tragic events of that February left Anne Shillitoe are not at all clear. Was it she who witnessed her mother praying for her accuser as she died? Had her father been there too at this time, before he determined to head out and hang himself? Whatever the exact circumstances, Shillitoe had lost both her parents in the most awful of situations and could possibly, at this time, still have faced an appearance at the York Assizes. But the conclusion of the legal case against the Denby 'witches', which had by then dragged on for at least six months, is unclear. The Surtees Society summary of York depositions suggests that the Assize records offer no information as to how it terminated and that "The deposition itself is torn in two, which seems to show that the matter came to nothing."[283] While they could have been referring to another deposition concerning this case where copies no longer exist, the original depositions held by the National Archives all appear completely intact, although none of them contain any evidence whatsoever of the Assizes' decision.

15. Post-scriptum

It is probably important to note that, while there were a large number of local people assigning their names in support of Hinchliffe and Shillitoe, clearly a large number of others did not, for whatever reason. Some will not have been approached by those organising it, as their sympathies may have been known to lie elsewhere. It is noticeable that, at a time of widespread illiteracy and the use of 'marks' to evidence identity, as Timothy Haigh did on his deposition, all those signing it did so with their names. There were clearly some less well-off who put their names to it but was the reason the petition contained no 'marks' because of a deliberate attempt to ensure it was made up of people with known local influence and standing?

We have no formal evidence, other than the depositions supportive of Mary Moor, to suggest that there was any groundswell of local opinion in her favour. We do not know if there was informal contact with the magistrates which persuaded them of the merits of the accusations. While the petition certainly raised questions about Moor's character, were the magistrates offered an alternative assessment of her merits which never became part of the limited formal record of the case?

There is little doubt that word of this case had spread far beyond the lanes and tracks of Over and Nether Denby, with the petition offering solid evidence of this. While the events of February, 1674/5, occurred during the depths winter, it would not be long before word of the deaths of Susanna and Joseph – and their circumstances – spread around the neighbourhood and beyond. Heywood's diary record of what happened suggests a continuing sympathy for the accused but, as the autumn and winter of 1674/5 wore on and there was no sign of the charges against them being dropped, despite a public outcry, did that sympathy possibly lessen? Was there less animosity towards Moor over what she had alleged?

If this scenario was re-run in contemporary society, particularly with the presence and contribution of 'social media', the likelihood would be – at the very least – threats of violence towards the accuser when the whole affair had ended in such tragedy. If Susanna's apparently final act, according to Heywood, of praying for Moor was true, did that have some influence on a wider view of the conclusion of the affair? There is no specific evidence that the Hinchliffes and Shillitoe subscribed to the clearly growing influence of Quaker theology within the wider Penistone parish at the time of the case but did its increasing prevalence have a bearing, in particular, on Mary Moor being able to get on with the rest of her life? What happened to her subsequently and whether she remained 'tainted' by the case is not known. She seems to have continued through life leaving no trace of her footsteps, but some might say she had already more than left her mark.

But as Moor and the events of 1674/5 gradually faded from living memory in Denby and the wider Penistone parish, unlike her, some of the key participants in the affair did continue to feature within the historic record for a variety of reasons. Jasper Blythman's ongoing magisterial role is evidenced by the record of his witnessing a sworn affidavit during August, 1678, to the effect that a William Silverwood had been buried "... in a shroud of woollen only."[284] The Burial in Wool Acts of 1667 and 1668, aimed at supporting the wool trade, had required a relative of the deceased to formally swear that a 'woollen burial' had taken place, with the significant sanction of a £5 fine being levied on the estate of those buried or their family for a breach of the law.

Blythman's connections with the extensive Wentworth family are illustrated by his direct involvement in another case which came to the attention of the York Assizes. On 18 January, 1681/2, he was involved in a game of cards at the Sign of The Angel pub, in Doncaster, when one of the participants, Thomas Maddox, the town's deputy postmaster, was killed. The man accused of his murder was Alexander Montgomerie, who had married Grace Popeley, the widow of Sir Thomas Wentworth of Bretton, in 1675, and was resident at Bretton at the time. Montgomerie, the Eighth Earl of Eglinton, had been found guilty and sentenced to death for the offence but, following a petition for leniency to King Charles II, later set free.[285]

There also would appear to have been some involvement of Jasper Blythman in the case of the former Holmfirth curate, Edmund Robinson. The churchman's notorious coining and counterfeiting activities primarily centred on his home at Bank End, between Brockholes and Thurstonland, and had started coming to light around the same time as the Denby witchcraft allegations in 1674. During January, 1679, he also was accused of having used witchcraft to detail exactly where some stolen items of clothing and linen were to be found.[286] After Robinson was found guilty of the treasonable offence of counterfeiting the King's coin on 23 March, 1690/1 and hanged at York, Blythman was one of the justices involved in an inquisition into his estate, held in Leeds on 21 September, 1692.[287]

Blythman's fellow magistrate, Charles Osborne, seems to have spent much of the rest of his life rather in the shadow of his older brother, Thomas, who, it has been suggested, "...as Earl of Danby had been the greatest figure after the monarch during the 1670s."[288] He had been Lord President of the Council and subsequently was made Duke of Leeds, while Charles, who died, unmarried, during 1719 at the ripe old age of 86, had, as has already been noted, the lesser distinction of being an MP, representing Hull.

George Sedascue's life ended at Heath (Old) Hall, near Wakefield, and he was buried at nearby Normanton on 4 December, 1688, aged 76. He appears to have remained at Gunthwaite Hall until well into his seventies and Dransfield describes the Hall as his address in detailing the legacy of £20 in his will to the Master of Penistone Grammar School, funding that was eventually used towards the erection of their house at the school.[289] A draft Assignment and Letter of Attorney dated 1684 seems to indicate that Sedascue was resident at Heath by then.[290]

Fig. 27. Heath Old Hall. (Green, 1889)

While some connections between Warmfield-cum-Heath and individuals featuring in the 1674 Denby case have been outlined in some detail, it is not immediately obvious why Sedascue's life should conclude at Heath rather than Gunthwaite. The longstanding occupant of the Old Hall, Lady Mary Bolles, whose father, William Witham, reputedly succumbed to 'witchcraft',[291] had died there, aged 83, during 1662, more than a decade before Sedascue signed the Denby petition. While Bolles's receipt of a baronetcy from Charles 1 in 1635 seems to suggest the likelihood of staunch Royalist credentials during the later Civil Wars period, she was subject to speculation that her generous entertaining of members of Wakefield's Royalist garrison at Heath on 20 May, 1643, led directly to the capturing of the city by Sir Thomas Fairfax's Parliamentary troops.

While Sedascue served under the command of Fairfax and would have known him, it is less likely he knew Bolles but it is worth noting that in her will, dated 4 May, 1662, a Daniel Oley is among those required to administer a substantial sum of money "to be paid to the Ministers of Wakefield".[292] His residence at Eshald House at Heath and the connection between the Oleys and Thomas Shillitoe has previously been mentioned in the context of land connected with the Shillitoes, near Cawthorne.

Sir William Dalston, having married Bolles' daughter, Anne, in 1635, appears to have occupied the Hall until his death in 1683 when, according to 'Lady' Green's 1889 account, it then passed into the ownership of Sir Charles Dalston, Bolles' great-grandson.[293] The complex arrangements of Heath Old Hall's inheritance have been outlined in detail by J. W. Walker in his Wakefield history and he evidenced it ending up in the hands of Anne, the third daughter of Sir Michael Wentworth of Woolley[294] and his wife, the former Dorothy Copley of Sprotborough. Anne was, of course, the granddaughter of the John Wentworth who appears to have the strongest claim to being the key magistrate dealing with Hinchliffe and Shillitoe.

Fig. 28. The elevated position of Heath Old Hall, viewed from alongside the River Calder downstream from Wakefield's Chantry Bridge. (Green, 1889)

Sedascue's eventual arrival at Heath Old Hall is – at least in part – explained by documents held by the National Archives relating to a quite extraordinary dispute which occurred over his will and came before the Lord High Commissioners for the Custody of the Great Seats of England during 1691. There is very limited information about what appears to be a diocesan court dealing with probate matters but submissions to it also clarify the detail of the parties involved and the issues in dispute. The statement of the plaintiff, dated 3 July, 1691, indicates that he was "...William Bossevile of Heath, in the County of York, gentleman, executor of the last will and testament of George Sedascue of Heath...".[295] William Bosville was the younger brother of Godfrey of Gunthwaite, for whom Sedascue and George Barnby had acted in estate matters until he came of age. The executor of the will was, therefore, Sedascue's nephew by marriage and appears to have accommodated him at Heath Old Hall at the time of his death.

But the statement also makes clear that, before he came to live at the Old Hall, Sedascue had been living less than two miles to the north east of Heath, at Newland. His residence there, at an estate close to the river Calder, with medieval connections to the Knights Templars and later the Knights Hospitallers, is explained by the marriage, in 1664, of William's sister, Mary Bosville, to "Edmund Bunny of, of Newland, esq."[296] The Bunny family had acquired the estate in 1546 and held it until 1694.[297] From the evidence put forward by William Bosville, it would seem that Sedascue had moved from Newland to Heath around 1683, which suggests that Bosville may have commenced occupation of the Old Hall as a consequence of the death of Sir William Dalston during that same year.

The key defendant in the case was a Margaret Lambert of Wakefield who had been working for Sedascue as his servant during the final years of his life. Following his death in 1688, Lambert had married a Joseph Shillitoe of Whitwood. I have established no direct connection between him and the Shillitoes involved with the Denby case and the common surname seems likely to have been a coincidence. He was named as a co-defendant, along with a Thomas Walker of Wakefield who was deemed to have owed monies to Sedascue at the time of his death.

Fig. 29. Newland Hall.
(The John Goodchild Collection, West Yorkshire Archive Service)

Central to Bosville's action was his allegation that Lambert had removed from the Old Hall several trunks containing numerous valuables as well as cash, but the central concern was they also held account books and documents without which it would be impossible for him to fulfil his role as sole executor. Complicating the situation was Margaret Lambert's claim that Sedascue had promised to marry her "... and that therefore she had a right to the testator's goods and ought to keep the same towards satisfaction for his breach of his said promise."[298]

While the question of why George Sedascue's life ended at Heath Old Hall, via Newland, might be answered by the connections with the Bosvilles evidenced in the will dispute, the reasons for his final resting place being Normanton are not entirely clear. Heath Old Hall lay within the parish of Warmfield-cum-Heath and it might have been expected he would, therefore, be buried at the parish church in Kirkthorpe, while his previous connections with Gunthwaite would have explained an alternate burial at Denby or Penistone. Margaret Lambert's alleged claim of his promise to marry her suggests he was a widower by the time of his residence at Heath Old Hall but locating a burial record for Mary Sedascue has not been possible. Could she have moved with him to live with Mary and Edmund Bunny at Newland, ending her life there? Newland lay within the Normanton parish and there is a record of "Mary Bunny of Nuland" being buried at Normanton on 12 February, 1694/5. It is possible that Mary Sedascue had previously been buried there, which is why that was also his final resting place.

It is noteworthy that the joint statement of defence from Margaret Shillitoe (nee Lambert), her husband Joseph and Thomas Walker made no mention of Sedascue's supposed promise of marriage and strongly refuted William Bosville's allegations that Margaret removed the deceased's monies or valuables and held keys to trunks containing them. She recalled being in Sedascue's room some time before he died, along with Bosville's wife, Benedicta, when the key to his study, containing his possessions, was in the door. On Benedicta's instructions, she had removed the key, passing it to William Bosville about an hour after Sedascue's death. The eventual outcome of this long and complicated dispute is not entirely clear but the Latin term "sarcio defendant"[299] in the Commissioners' documents would seem to suggest that the Shillitoes and Walker may have been ordered to make amends and somehow recompense Bosville. But it is quite striking that, even after the end of his long and very eventful life, George Sedascue remained in the spotlight.

The Denby witchcraft case would have been a very minor chapter in the old soldier's many years as it would also have been for the preacher, Oliver Heywood, a central figure in ensuring there was some outline record of the whole story. It is difficult to verify or date a suggestion that Heywood himself actually, at one point, also became the subject of a witchcraft allegation. The context was that it was not uncommon for dissenters, like him, to be subject to accusations and rumours which were designed to cast doubt upon their validity as preachers. An article on "Witchcraft in 17th Century Northowram" implies that gossip emerged from "...the Rastrick house of a rival minister by the name of John Hanson..." where it had been suggested people steered clear of Heywood's Coley home "...for fear of witches." Specifically, it was claimed that the wife of a man by the name of Jagger had been noted departing Heywood's home one evening "...during which time she was supposed to have 'got power' over a maid of Anthony Waterhouse. The servant girl was soon 'distempered and strangely taken' and in her delirium claimed to see the apparition of Jagger's wife. She died within a fortnight."[300]

Heywood makes no mention of this alleged episode in his own published diaries, anecdotes and event books, but his life in the years following the Denby allegations certainly contained its challenges. One of his many battles with the religious authorities resulted in him spending 1685 imprisoned in York Castle. Describing his imprisonment for conscience' sake, Fletcher suggests "...he took his affliction with a good spirit, as being part of a necessary earthly experience."[301]

And, over a century and a half on from Heywood's important account of the event, the first national census recording the personal detail obtained by the enumerators, in 1841, noted a Shillitoe family still resident in the Denby township. In the context of previously noting the Shillitoes' possible links with "Rowleys", near Cawthorne, the likelihood of their having resided some way to the east of Denby has already been considered. At the time of the census, headed by another Thomas and his wife, Rachel, along with their five children, they were farming at Upper Bagden,[302] where the old lane from Denby Hall Farm joins the road from High Hoyland to Denby, just to the east of Pool Hill. The 1851 census describes Thomas as a farmer of 20 acres and, while the two returns differ on the year, between 1804 and 1806, the later one records his place of birth as Denby.

The Penistone parish registers detail the marriage of a Thomas Shillito and Rachel Hatfield on 12 April, 1830, but while the 1851 census records Rachel Shillito's place of birth as Cawthorne, the most likely baptismal record for her is at the Netherfield (Independent) Chapel, at Thurlstone, near Penistone, on 21 April, 1807.

16. Another of these strange cases...

I made clear at the start of this book that it wasn't my intention to try to examine the circumstances of the Denby allegations alongside the numerous theories put forward to explain so-called 'witchcraft' in its various manifestations. My purpose has been to focus on the 1674 case as a means of trying to gain a better understanding of the local community affected by its significance at the time. David and Andrew Pickering's study of English witchcraft pinpoints the fact that most of the allegations about it arose in exactly the kind of small rural community in which Hinchliffe and Shillitoe lived: "In these intimate environments there was none of the anonymity that could be found in urban settings. Everyone knew each other's business and life history. Affection and enmity among neighbours could build up over long periods of time. Here...the conservative, illiterate peasantry held fast to old beliefs and suspicions, including, perhaps, a belief in witchcraft."[303]

These wider points may well have obvious relevance, but it is important, too, to perhaps give some thought to what really lay behind these particular accusations which so obviously concluded in awful tragedy. We know they primarily concerned the claims of a 16-year-old girl made against two older females. The detail of these claims, when viewed from a 21st century perspective, appear utterly far-fetched and, frankly, ridiculous, but clearly resonated at a time when witchcraft was widely believed to be prevalent and a threat to society. The Denby case was a by no means isolated incident and James Sharpe's examination of this case' and others featuring on the Northern assize circuit during the second half of the 17th century, offers an important key theme which, perhaps, rather cuts through a lot of the other complex explanations which may be on offer. "As the high percentage of women victims and witnesses in the Yorkshire sample suggests, many of the incidents which led to an allegation of witchcraft involved tensions between women."[304] Similarly, in her analysis of the first of many witchcraft trials, Willow Winsham states that "As was so often the case, it started with a simple feud between two women."[305]

A continuing local reminder of the locality's past response to what were deemed 'scolding' women is Cuckstool Bridge over the River Dearne, just down Miller Hill from Lower Denby, in what is nowadays Denby Dale. The so-called cucking stool would have punished them by being strapped to a wooden contraption and lowered into the water. Frank Peel's description of their purpose is more than a little dated but perhaps very much reflects the thinking from the times they were in use. They were, he suggests, seen as "...a fitting punishment for women who by their mischievous tongues often wrecked the peace of families and wrought mischief which could never be repaired simply to gratify their revengeful feelings, or in too many cases, from a pure love of gossip and scandal."[306]

At a time when religious affiliation was a fundamental part of social relationships at a local level were differences in belief a factor in what happened? Holly Bamford, a Liverpool University PhD student, studying 'community dynamics' in witchcraft trials has raised this possibility in the Denby case, particularly questioning whether Mary Moor might have somehow been rejected by the local Presbyterians. Her interest in the specifics of 1674 relate in particular to the rarity of a local population apparently rallying in support of accused witches and Susanna Hinchliffe obviously being anything but the social outcast who is usually under suspicion.[307] But if religious differences did play a part in these developments, it is not at all clear why the Hinchliffes and their daughter should have been the apparent focus of Moor's attention.

The recent revival of Arthur Miller's play 'The Crucible' raises another, perhaps less plausible, possibility. Using the 1692 Salem witch trials as an allegory for what he saw as the anti-communist hysteria of his day in the USA, it tells the story of a teenage girl who accuses her married lover's wife of witchcraft in order to be rid of her, so they can continue their affair. While Mary Moor's motives in the Denby case are a matter of speculation, it is noticeable that Thomas Shillitoe was the only member of the extended family against whom she did not make allegations of witchcraft.

As in Miller's play, events in Denby unfolded as a direct consequence of what seem to be the malicious accusations of a teenager. The petition informs us that Mary Moor was not held in high esteem by many of those living nearby. Perhaps they shunned or even scolded her, but people were listening to her. The more fanciful the stories she told, the more attention she received, and she may well have found this addictive and flattering.

We shall never know exactly what might have caused possible tensions between Hinchliffe, Shillitoe and Moor, or whether these also involved some of the other parties from the locality who feature in the depositions concerning the case. The fact that detail within Moor's depositions evidence that the plaintiff and the accused were, at least at one point, on good enough terms to agree the loan of a line wheel suggests relations had been reasonable enough. If they had fallen out, it is impossible to establish exactly why, but Sharpe's evaluation of the common causal factors behind allegations may have direct relevance to the Denby case. While patriarchal and misogynistic male attitudes were often cited in order to understand accusations, "...on a village level witchcraft seems to have been something peculiarly enmeshed in women's quarrels and the way in which they settled them."[308] We are also unlikely to ever establish what was implied – but not specified - about Mary Moor's character in the wording of the petition in support of the accused. However, the totally unqualified endorsement offered by the overwhelming majority of signatories suggests that some possible flaws may have been known to them, even if they weren't to the examining magistrate. In Moor's defence, perhaps it should be noted that the petitioners were almost entirely male.

An interesting footnote to the Surtees Society record of the proceedings, published well over a century and a half ago, summed up what happened as "Another of these strange cases which occurred in the West Riding of Yorkshire."[309] And its author didn't beat about the bush in pointing the finger at Wentworth, Blythman and Osborne. "The evidence is plainly that of a malicious and ignorant person, and one would scarcely believe it possible that any magistrate would sit down to write such nonsense from the lips of anyone."[310] Eli Hoyle has suggested that Mary Moor "...bore an indifferent character..." with her extensive evidence being "...of the same childish kind." His conclusion was that "The whole case would have been laughable were it not for the tragedy in which the affair ended."[311] The Pickerings' detailed summary of the persecution of alleged witches also includes reference to the Denby case and their overall summary of the bizarre nature of so much that was going on has direct relevance. Making the point that, although witchcraft allegations accounted for a small minority of court cases in the early modern period "...this crime has received most attention both because of our enduring fascination with the supernatural, and also, when we see beyond the illusory magic, because of its apparent absurdity."[312]

So, even accepting the fact that attitudes towards 'witchcraft' in Early Modern England were a good deal less enlightened than those of today, bearing in mind that, as has been noted, by the latter half of the 17th century, prosecutions had fallen considerably from their peak in the last two decades of the 1500s, why was it that this case was referred to the Assizes rather than dismissed out of hand? What convinced Wentworth that Hinchliffe and Shillitoe apparently had powers to do harm and were, in fact, using those powers? Why did the magistrate determine that Moor's deposition warranted examination by a higher judicial authority with significantly greater powers than he had, including, of course, the ability to pass a death sentence on those found guilty? Why did he apparently have greater faith in Moor's portrayal of the accused than that of well over fifty local residents of some status who chose to testify to the character of Hinchliffe, in particular? And why did he determine to disregard the opinions of those residents as to the character and reliability of the one plaintiff in the case?

We do not know if Wentworth had particularly strong views on the notion of malefic acts but it has been suggested such magistrates "...shared the feelings about witchcraft of the class from which they were drawn, the country gentry, and such feelings might run from the very hostile to the very sceptical."[313] We know his parents had been staunch Roman Catholics. Whether he was a 'Church Papist' or not, had he grown up with the notion of the devil's emissaries at large in the local community? His actions might suggest a particular hostility, but was there some wider antagonism at play here within which Hinchliffe and Shillitoe were mere bit-part players? If there is an answer, then does it actually lie within the quite recent history of conflict which had bitterly divided both individual families and local communities in villages such as Denby, and parishes like Penistone, not many years earlier during the English Civil Wars? What stands out loud and clear from the petition put to the West Riding magistrates in support of the accused is that the signatories overwhelmingly stemmed from the ranks of those who had been sympathetic to and – in some cases – militarily active in support of the Parliamentary cause. Their names include those at the forefront of local Protestant dissent, several of whom were, or would go on to become, leading non-conformists. The supporters of the accused women were, in many instances, markedly different in outlook from the magistrates dealing with the case. It is not unreasonable to suggest that this remarkable petition of support for Susanna Hinchliffe and Anne Shillitoe may have had completely the opposite effect to that intended by the organisers and signatories.

Bibliography

Addy, J. (ed.) "The History of Denby Dale Parish." Denby Dale Parish Council, 1995.

Alliott, Gerald J. "The Vanishing Relics of Barnsley." Wharncliffe Publishing, 1996.

Bedford, Edward J. "Genealogical Memoranda relating to the Family of Wordsworth". Privately published, 1881.

Binns, Jack. "Yorkshire in the Civil Wars." Blackthorne Press, 2004.

Bower, David, and Knight, John. "Plain Country Friends". Wooldale Meeting of the Religious Society of Friends, 1987.

Catlow, Richard, "The Pendle Witches." Hendon, 1976.

Cliffe, J. T. "Yorkshire Gentry: from the Reformation to the Civil War." University of London, Athlone Press, 1969.

Cross, John. "The Curate and the King's Coin." Shalliley Books, 2019.

Crowther, George H. "A Descriptive History of the Wakefield Battles; and a short account of this Ancient and Important Town." W. Nicholson and Sons, 1886.

Downing, Taylor, and Millman, Maggie. "Civil War." B.C.A., 1992.

Dransfield, John N. "A History of the Parish of Penistone." J. H. Wood, 1906.

Elliott, Brian. "The Making of Barnsley." Wharncliffe Publishing Ltd., 1988.

Elliott, Brian, (ed.). "Aspects of Barnsley." Wharncliffe Books, 1993.

Fletcher, J. S. "Yorkshiremen in the Restoration." George Allen and Unwin, 1921.

Green, 'Lady'. "The Old Hall at Heath". W. H. Milnes, 1889.

Hall, Ivan and Elizabeth. "Heath: an Architectural Description." Muir and Mary Oddie, undated.

Heath, Chris. "Denebi – Farmstead of the Danes." Netherwood, 1997.

Heath, Chris. "Denby and District from Pre-history to the Present." Wharncliffe, 2001.

Heath, Chris. "Denby and District II: from Landed Lords to Inspired Industrialists." Wharncliffe, 2004.

Heath, Chris. "Denby and District III: from Medieval Manuscripts to Modern Memories." Pen & Sword, 2006.

Heath, Chris. "Denby and District IV: Chronicles of Clerics, Convicts, Corn Millers and Comedians." Pen & Sword, 2009.

Heath, Chris. "Denby Dale and Upper Denby: Unknown and Unseen." Pen & Sword, 2017.

Heath Residents Association. "The Time of Our Lives in Heath." HRA, 2000.

Hewitt, John. "History and Topography of the Parish Of Wakefield and its Environs." Unknown publisher, 1863.

Hey, David. "Yorkshire from AD 1000." Longman, 1986.

Hey, David. "The Oxford Companion to Local and Family History." Oxford University Press, 1996.

Hey, David. "A History of Penistone and District." Wharncliffe Books, 2002.

Hey, David. "Packmen, Carriers and Packhorse Roads." Landmark Publishing, 2004.

Hey, David. "A History of Yorkshire: 'County of the Broad Acres'." Carnegie, 2005.

Hey, David; Giles, Colum; Spufford, Margaret and Wareham, Andrew. "West Riding Hearth Tax." British Record Society, 2007.

Hinchliffe, David. "Descent into Silence: Cawthorne's Forgotten Tragedy." Scratching Shed, 2021.

Hoyle, Eli. "A History of Barnsley from Early Times to 1850. Vol. 1." Undated.

Humphery-Smith, Cecil R. "The Phillimore Atlas and Index of Parish Registers." Phillimore, 3rd edition, 2020.

Hunter, Joseph. "The Life Of Oliver Heywood." Originally published 1842. Undated reprint by Legare.

Hunter, Joseph. "South Yorkshire, Vols. I and II". 1828-31. Re-published by E.P. Publishing, 1974.

Jackson, Rowland. "The History of the Town and Township of Barnsley." London, Bell and Daldy, 1858.

Lawton, Fred. "Historical Notes of Skelmanthorpe and District." Originally published by Paul Dyson of Skelmanthorpe but reprinted by Denby Dale Civic Society, 1986.

Levack, Brian. "The Witch-hunt in Early Modern Europe." Routledge, 2015.

Markham, Leonard, ed. P. Norman. "Tales from West Yorkshire." Countryside Books, 1992.

Morehouse, H. J. "The History and Topography of the Parish of Kirkburton and the Graveship of Holme." 1861.

Morehouse, H. J. "Three Huddersfield Diaries." Toll House, 1990.

Morgan, Kenneth O. (ed.). "The Oxford Popular History of Britain." Paragon, 1998.

Peel, Frank. "Nonconformity in the Spen Valley". Senior, 1891.

Peel, Frank. "Spen Valley: Past and Present." Senior, 1893.

Pickering, David and Andrew. "Witch Hunt: The Persecution of Witches in England." Amberley, 2013.

Prince, Joseph. "The History and Topography of the Parish of Silkstone in the County of York." J. H. Wood, 1922.

Redmonds, George. "Huddersfield and District under the Stuarts: seventy years of law and disorder." GR Books, 1985.

Redmonds, George. "Christian Names in Local and Family History." National Archives, 2004.

Redmonds, George. "A Dictionary of Yorkshire Surnames." Shaun Tyas, 2015.

Redmonds, George, and Alexandra Medcalf (ed.). "The Yorkshire Historical Dictionary." Yorkshire Archaeological and Historical Society, 2021.

Rennison, Eileen. "Yorkshire Witches." Amberley, 2012.

Richards, Denis. "Britain under the Tudors and Stuarts". Longman, 1971.

Robinson, Leslie. "Remembering Marshall Mill, Scissett." Denby Dale Parish Council, 2010.

Sharpe, J. A. "Witchcraft in Seventeen Century Yorkshire: Accusations and Counter Measures." Borthwick Institute, 1992.

Sharpe, James. "Instruments of Darkness: Witchcraft in early Modern England." University of Pennsylvania Press, 1997.

Smith, D. J. "Aspects of Life in Old Cawthorne." Publisher and date unknown.

Smith, William (ed.). "Old Yorkshire." Longmans, Green, 1883.

Summers, Montague. "The History of Witchcraft and Demonology." Dover, 2007.

Tate, W. E. "The Parish Chest." Pub. Cambridge University Press, 1983.

Turner, J. Horsfall. "The Rev. Oliver Heywood, B.A.: His Autobiography, Diaries, Anecdote and Event Books." Originally published by A. B. Bayes, 1882. Reprint by Legare Street Press, undated.

Walker, J. W. "Wakefield: Its History and People." E.P. Publishing, 1939.

Walsham, Alexandra. "Church Papists, Catholicism, Conformity and Confessional Polemic in Early Modern England." Bodyell Press, 1993.

Whiteman, Ann and Mary Clapison (eds.). "The Compton Census of 1676." Oxford University Press, 1986.

Wilkinson, John. "Exploring the Upper Dearne Valley." Bridge, 2002.

Winsham, Willow. "England's Witchcraft Trials." Pen & Sword, 2018.

References

Isaac Penington [before introduction] From: Quaker faith and practice: the book of Christian discipline of the Yearly Meeting of the Religious Society of Friends (Quakers) in Britain." The Yearly Meeting of the Religious Society of Friends (Quakers) in Britain. Fourth edition, 2009. Para. 10.01.)

---

[1] Wheater, William, in Smith, William (ed.) "Old Yorkshire." Longmans, Green, 1883, p. 265.

[2] In 1645, Matthew Hopkins had secured for himself a Parliamentary Commission investigating 'witchcraft', which resulted in around 200 people, mainly women, dying in East Anglia before Hopkins himself was hung for sorcery in 1647.

[3] Smith, op cit. P 265.

[4] Ibid.

[5] Ibid.

[6] Morgan, Kenneth O. (ed). "The Oxford Popular History of Britain." Oxford University Press, 1993. P. 397.

[7] Levack, Brian P. "The Witch-hunt in Early Modern Europe." Routledge, 2015.

[8] Downing, Taylor and Millman, Maggie. "Civil War." BCA, 1992. P. 153.

[9] Ibid.

[10] Peel, Frank. "Spen Valley: Past and Present." Senior, 1893. P. 170.

[11] Ibid.

[12] Downing and Millman, op. cit. P. 164.

[13] Crossland, Phyllis. "Old Yorkshire." Issue 21. Winter 2001. P. 10.

[14] Hey, David; Giles, Colum; Spufford, Margaret and Wareham, Andrew. "West Riding Hearth Tax." British Record Society, 2007, p.373/4.

[15] Hey in Hey et al (2007), op. cit., suggests a notional average household size of between 4.25 and 4.75 has often been used as a multiplier to estimate population levels.

[16] Hey et al (2007), op cit.

[17] Summers, Montague. "The History of Witchcraft and Demonology." Dover, 2007. (First published, 1926). P. ix.

[18] Sharpe, James. "Instruments of Darkness: Witchcraft in Early Modern England." University of Pennsylvania, 1997. P. 163.q

[19] Hey et al (2007), op. cit.

[20] Morrill, John, in Morgan, Kenneth O. "The Oxford Popular History of Britain". Oxford University Press, 1988. P. 331.

[21] Hey, D. "A History of Penistone and District." Wharncliffe Books, 2002, p.136/7.
   Crowther, G. H. "A Descriptive History of the Wakefield Battles and a short account of this Ancient and Important Town." W. Nicholson and Sons, 1886. NB I

am indebted to Sue and Geoff Wake for the loan of their copy of this book. It is their understanding that the handwritten notes may have been added by Crowther himself, suggesting that their copy was originally owned by the author.

[22] Fletcher, J.S. "Yorkshiremen in the Restoration." George Allen and Unwin, 1921. P. 172.

[23] Hewitt, John. "The John Hewitt Collection, 1860-1881". Wakefield Libraries and Local Studies. Ref. 427:WAK.

[24] Pickering, David and Andrew. "Witch Hunt: The Persecution of Witches in England." Amberley, 2013. P. 213. The Pickerings refer to Rev. J. Hunter's "The Life Of Oliver Heywood", pub. 1842.

[25] Peel, op. cit. P.406.

[26] Fletcher, op. cit. P.180.

[27] Ibid. P. 176/7.

[28] Turner, J. Horsfall. "The Rev. Oliver Heywood, B.A.: His Autobiography, Diaries, Anecdote and Event Books." Originally published by A. B. Bayes, 1882. Reprint by Legare Street Press, undated, p. 362.

[29] Hey, et al (2007), op. cit. P. 373.

[30] "Subsidy Roll (Poll Tax) for 1379 for the Yorkshire Parish of Emley." Transcribed from Yorkshire Archaeological and Topographical Journals in 2001. On-line source.

[31] Ibid.

[32] Hey, et al (2007), op. cit. P. 376.

[33] Ibid. P. 316.

[34] A William Hynchclyff of Woolley features in 1430 in the will of an Oliver Woderow. YAS Vol. 66. P. 66.

[35] Elliott, Brian. "Barnsley: the anatomy of a Yorkshire market town and its neighbourhood C1660-C1760." M.Phil, thesis. University of Sheffield. June, 1990. P. 56.

[36] Hey, et al (2007), op. cit. P. 381.

[37] Ibid. Ps. 373, 372, 244.

[38] Pickering, op. cit. P. 213.

[39] Heath, Chris. "Denby & District from Pre-history to the Present." Wharncliffe Books, 1997. P. 109.

[40] Rennison, Eileen. "Yorkshire Witches." Amberley, 2012. P. 17.

[41] Markham, Leonard. "Tales from West Yorkshire." Countryside Books, 1992. P. 49.

[42] Hoyle, Eli. "A History of Barnsley from Early times to 1850". Ed. Phil Norman. Vol. 1. P. 403.

[43] Pavers Marriage Licences. Vol. 2. 1660-1674. Yorkshire Archaeological Society.

[44] Hey, David. "The Oxford Companion to Local and Family History." Oxford University Press, 1996. P. 509.

[45] YAS Vol. 66. P. 66.

[46] Jackson, Rowland. "The History of the Town and Township of Barnsley." London: Bell and Daldy, 1858. P. 109.

[47] Humphery-Smith, Cecil R. "Atlas and Index of Parish Registers." Phillimore, 3rd edition, 2020. Map 6G (B).

[48] Commonwealth Probate Index, 1654/5. P. 215.

[49] Hall, Ivan and Elizabeth. "Heath: an Architectural Description". Oddie. Undated. P. 13.

[50] Morehouse, H. J. 'The Journal or Diary of Captain Adam Eyre' in "Three Huddersfield Diaries." Toll House, 1990. P. 22.

[51] Hey, et al (2007), op. cit. P. 296.

[52] Commonwealth Probate Index 1654/5. P. 215.

[53] Spencer Stanhope Archive, Barnsley (subsequently Sp. St.). 60321/139.

[54] Sp. St. 60376/194/8.

[55] Sp. St. 60376/194/9.

[56] Smith, D. J. "Aspects of Life in Old Cawthorne, South Yorkshire." Hilltop Press, 1970. P. 9.

[57] The 1851 census returns record a Thomas Shillito (born 1807), a farmer of 20 acres, as resident at Upper Bagden.

[58] West Yorkshire Archive Service ref. WYHER 9474/MWY 6568.Hey

[59] Heath, Chris. "Denby and District 111: from Medieval Manuscripts to Modern Memories." Wharncliffe, 2006. P. 23.

[60] Dransfield, John N. "History of Penistone". James H. Wood, 1906. P. 11.

[61] Sp. St. 60275 90/13.

[62] Heath (2006), op. cit. P. 24.

[63] Sp. St. 60321 139/25a.

[64] Hey, et al (2007), op. cit. Ps.376 and 381.

[65] Redmonds, George. "Christian Names in Local and Family History." National Archives, 2004. P. 21, where the author quotes research published in 1997 by Scott Smith-Bannister.

[66] Ibid.

[67] Wilkinson, John. "Exploring the Upper Dearne Valley." Bridge, 2002. P. 83.

[68] Heath, (1997), op. cit. P. 179.

[69] Morehouse, op. cit. P. 87.

[70] Hey, et al (2007), op. cit. P. 373.

[71] Heath, Chris. "Denebi: Farmstead of the Danes." Richard Netherwood, 1997. P. 46.

[72] Redmonds, (2004), op. cit. P. 161.

[73] Redmonds, George, ed. Medcalf, Alexandra. "The Yorkshire Historical Dictionary." Yorkshire Archaeological and Historical Society, 2021. P.680.

[74] Lawton, Fred. "Historical Notes of Skelmanthorpe and District." Originally published by Paul Dyson (date unknown) and reprinted by Denby Dale Civic Society, 1986. P. 18. Heath, Chris."Denebi: Farmstead of the Danes." Netherwood, 1997. P. 45.

[75] Bower, David and Knight, John. "Plain Country Friends: The Quakers of Wooldale, High Flatts and Midhope." Wooldale Meeting of the Religious Society of Friends, 1987. P. 145.

[76] Heath, (1997), op. cit. P. 71.

[77] Hey, (2002), op. cit. P.59/60.

[78] Pickering, op. cit. P. 213.

[79] Hey, et al (2007), op. cit. P. 380/1.

[80] Ibid. P.356.

[81] Hey, et al (2007), op. cit. P. 376.

[82] Ibid. P 247.

[83] Catlow, Richard. "The Pendle Witches". Hendon, 1976. P. 6.

[84] Winsham, Willow. "England's Witchcraft Trials." Pen and Sword, 2018. P.51.

[85] ASSI 45/11/1. National Archives.

[86] Ibid.

[87] Tate, W. E. "The Parish Chest". Cambridge University Press, 1983. P. 177.

[88] Hey, (1996), op. cit. P. 109.

[89] Binns, Jack. "Yorkshire in the Civil Wars." Blackthorn Press, 2004. P.3.

[90] "Depositions from the Castle of York relating to Offences Committed in the Northern Counties in the Seventeenth Century". Vol. XL. Surtees Society, London, 1861. P. 208.

[91] Lawton, op. cit. P. 17.

[92] Hoyle, op. cit. Vol 1. P. 403.

[93] For example, Chris Heath in "Denebi: Farmstead of the Danes" (Netherwood, 1997, p. 44) and "Denby and District: From Pre-History to the present" (Wharncliffe Books, 1997, p. 108), as well as Brian Elliott in "The Making of Barnsley" (Wharncliffe Books, 1988, p. 248).

[94] Rennison, op. cit. P. 50.

[95] "Restoring character to house that dates from the 1600s." Yorkshire Post, 8 March, 2014.

[96] Hunter, Joseph. "South Yorkshire". Nichols and Son, 1828-31 (republished by EP Publishing Ltd., 1974). Vol 2, p. 78.

[97] Ibid. P. 315.

[98] Hey, et al (2007), op. cit. P. 381.

[99] Ibid. Ps. 592, 594 and 598.

[100] Leeds University Library Special Collections. Ref. Wentworth – Woolley Hall/10.

[101] Binns, op. cit. P. 47.

[102] Ibid. P. 119.

[103] Taylor, Kate. Ed. 'Research throws fresh light on Woolley Hall' in "Wakefield District Heritage", Wakefield European Archaeological Year Committee, 1976. P. 6.

[104] Ibid. P. 181.

[105] Hoyle, op. cit. Vol. 1. P. 387.

[106] Humphrey, Jean. "Wentworth Castle: A Short History." Publisher and date unknown.

[107] "Dugdale's Visitation of Yorkshire". Vol. 2. Pollard, 1907. P.323.

[108] Cliffe, J.T. "The Yorkshire Gentry: from the Reformation to the Civil War." University of London, Athlone Press, 1969. P. 189.

[109] Ibid. P. 344.

[110] See Walsham , Alexandra. "Church Papists: Catholicism, Conformity and Confessional Polemic in early Modern England." Bodyell Press, 1993.

[111] Jackson, op. cit. P. 131.

[112] ASSI 45/11/1. National Archives.

[113] Sedbergh School Register. On-line source.

[114] Ibid.

[115] Jackson, op. cit. P. 242.

[116] Morehouse, op. cit. Ps 45, 47 and 83.

[117] Ibid. Ps. 24/25.

[118] Dransfield, op. cit. P. 11.

[119] Hey, et al (2007), op. cit. Ps.371 and 427.

[120] Ibid. P.594.

[121] ASSI 45/11/1. National Archives.

[122] On line source.http://www.j31/dukeof leeds.html

[123] On line source. http://www.british.library.ac.uk/report

[124] Elliott, (1988) op. cit. P. 248.

[125] Hester, Marianne, quoted in Sharpe, op. cit. P. 169.

[126] Alliott, Gerald. "Prisons and Courts in Barnsley". Journal of Barnsley Family History Society, January, 2001.

[127] Ibid.

[128] Pickering, op. cit. P. 14.

[129] Sharpe, op. cit. P. 165.

[130] Ibid. P. 167.

[131] Lawton, op. cit. P. 19.

[132] Hoyle, op. cit. P.403.

[133] ASSI 45/11/1. National Archives.

[134] Morehouse, op. cit.

[135] Hey, (2002) op. cit. P. 84.

[136] Dransfield, op. cit. Ps. 17 and 47.

[137] His distinctive handwriting has, for example, been noted on the 1698 petition concerning Penistone market. See Hey, 2002, op cit. Ps. 98-100.

[138] On-line source. "Soldiers of the Civil War: George Sedascue" by Barry Denton. In 'English Civil War Notes And Queries", Issue 1, ps. 5-6.

[139] Dransfield, op. cit. P. 85.

[140] Ibid. P. 18.

[141] House of Commons Journal. Vol 7. 11 January, 1660.

[142] Gentles, Ian. "The New Model Army Officer Corps in 1647: a Collective Portrait," in Social History Vol. 22, 1997. Issue 2.

[143] Hey, D. G. in Northern History, Vol. XXX1. P. 181.

[144] Nicholson, Vera, in Elliott, Brian (Ed.) "Aspects of Barnsley". Wharncliffe Books, 1993. P. 212.

[145] Ibid. P. 212.

[146] Morehouse, op. cit. P. 26.

[147] Dransfield, op. cit. P. 28.

[148] Ibid. P. 28.

[149] Hey, et al (2007), op. cit. P. 373.

[150] Hunter, op. cit. P. 233.

[151] Prince, Joseph. "The History and Topography of the Parish of Silkstone in the County of York". J.H. Wood, 1922. P. 157.

[152] Sp. St. 60255/70.

[153] Known as the Compton Census, after Henry Compton, then Bishop of London.

[154] See Whiteman, Ann and Clapinson, Mary (eds). "The Compton Census of 1676: A Critical Edition." Oxford University Press, 1986.

[155] Sp. St. 60187/7. Dowell Bank was probably what is now known as Daw Walls on the Lane Head Road, near Cawthorne.

[156] Hey, et al (2007), op. cit. P. 371.

[157] Sp. St. 60298 113/1-19 & 60366 184/11/12/13.

[158] Hey, et al (2007), op. cit. P. 376.

[159] Morehouse, op. cit.

[160] Hey, et al (2007), op. cit. P. 376.

[161] Bower, and Knight, op. cit. Ps. 127-131.

[162] Addy, J. (ed.). "The History of Denby Dale Parish." Denby Dale Parish Council, 1995. P. 23.

[163] Ibid.

[164] Dransfield, op. cit. P. 171.

[165] Hey, et al (2007), op. cit. P. 376.

[166] Redmonds, George. "A Dictionary of Yorkshire Surnames." Shaun Tyas, 2015. P. 509.

[167] Ibid.

[168] Hey, 2002, op. cit. P. 55.

[169] Hunter, op. cit. Vol. 2. P. 353.

[170] Hey, et al (2007), op. cit. P. 376.

[171] Morehouse, op. cit. P. 50.

[172] Ibid. P. 31.

[173] Ibid. P. 80.

[174] Hey, et al (2007), op. cit. P. 376.

[175] Morehouse, op. cit. P. 30.

[176] Dransfield, op. cit. P. 33.

[177] Ibid.
[178] Hey, et al (2007), op. cit. P. 213.
[179] The 1584 will of Richard Kent of Leeds evidences a family connection with the Foxcrofts, who were major players in the early industrialisation of Leeds. See Genuki: Leeds Wills Index. On-line source.
[180] Global Christian Leaders Index. On-line source.
[181] Sp. St. 60411 228/3/1.
[182] Sp. St. 60329/147.
[183] Sp. St. 60411 228/3/2.
[184] Sp. St. 60411 228/5.
[185] Hey (2002). op. cit. P.79.
[186] Hunter, op. cit. Vol 2. P. 350.
[187] Sp. St. 60402 219/1 and 3.
[188] See Redmonds, George. "Christian Names in Local and Family History". National Archives, 2004. Ps. 71-72.
[189] Op. cit. P. 72.
[190] Hey, et al (2007), op. cit. P. 373.
[191] Jackson, op. cit. P. 36.
[192] Hey, et al (2007), op. cit. P. 373.
[193] Hunter, op. cit. Vol. 2. P. 351.
[194] Ibid.
[195] Prince, op. cit. P. 172.
[196] Redmonds, (2015) op. cit. P. 153.
[197] Sp. St. 60329 147/1.
[198] Dransfield, op. cit. P. 11.
[199] Sp. St. 60351 169/1/2; 64755/45.
[200] Redmonds, George. "A Dictionary of Yorkshire Surnames." Shaun Tyas, 2015. P. 688.
[201] Turner, op. cit. Ps. 233,234,242, 243, 270, 360.
[202] Hey, et al (2007), op. cit. P. 375.
[203] Turner, op. cit. P. 234.
[204] Turner, op. cit. P. 270.
[205] Bower and Knight, op. cit. P. 9.
[206] Hey, David. "Packmen, Carriers and Packhorse Roads." Landmark Publishing, 2004. P. 48.
[207] Sp. St. 60329/147.
[208] Ibid.
[209] Hey et al (2007), op. cit. P. 375.
[210] See Sp. St. 60329 147, dated 24/5/1673.
[211] Morehouse, op. cit.
[212] Richards, Denis. "Britain under the Tudors and Stuarts". Longman, 1971. P. 275.
[213] Turner, op. cit. P. 360.

[214] Ibid.

[215] Morehouse, op. cit. P. 18.

[216] Ibid. See Ps. 65, 70, 74, 98, 117 and 122.

[217] Bedford, Edwin J. "Genealogical Memoranda relating to the Family of Wordsworth". Privately published, 1881.

[218] Hey et al (2007), op. cit. P. 377.

[219] Bedford, op. cit.

[220] Will of Ambrose Wordsworth of Schole Hill. Copy held by Heritage Silkstone.

[221] Dransfield, op. cit. P. 3.

[222] Turner, op. cit. Ps. 233, 244, 250, 264 and 270.

[223] Sp. St. 60404 221/2.

[224] Prince, op. cit. P. 34.

[225] Turner, op. cit. P. 250.

[226] Ibid. P. 270.

[227] Ibid. P. 288.

[228] Hey, (2002), op. cit. P. 94.

[229] Dransfield, op. cit. P. 14.

[230] Turner, op. cit. P. 306.

[231] Hey, (2002), op. cit. P. 84.

[232] Turner, op. cit. P. 188.

[233] Dransfield, op. cit. P. 66.

[234] Sp. St. 60236 51/20.

[235] See Sp. St. 60182/29, 60188/3, 60236/51, 60240/51, 64691/2, and 64713 1/2.

[236] Sp. St. 60411 228/2.

[237] Morehouse, op. cit. Ps. 19/20.

[238] Hey et al (2007). P. 373.

[239] Ibid. P. 379.

[240] Ibid. P. 374.

[241] Bower and Knight, op. cit. P. 7.

[242] Hey et al (2007), op. cit. P. 373.

[243] Bower and Knight, op. cit. P. 145.

[244] Ibid.

[245] Hey et al (2007), op. cit. P. 381.

[246] Bower and Knight, op. cit. P. 150.

[247] Ibid.

[248] Redmonds, George. "Huddersfield and District under the Stuarts: Seventy years of Law and Disorder." GR Books, 1985. P. 41.

[249] Hey et al (2007), op. cit. P 381.

[250] Dransfield, op. cit. P. 49.

[251] Redmonds, op. cit. P. 300.

[252] Sp. St. 60411 228/2.

[253] Hey et al (2007), op. cit. P. 374.

[254] Ibid. P. 435.

[255] Referred to in Robert Blackburne will dated 29/3/1680. Sp. St. 60447 265/3.

[256] Dransfield, op. cit. P. 35.

[257] Ibid. P. 198.

[258] Ibid.

[259] Hey et al (2007), op. cit. P. 377.

[260] Dransfield, op. cit. P. 198.

[261] Ibid. P. 381.

[262] Ibid. P. 373.

[263] Ibid. P. 381.

[264] Heath (1997), op. cit. P. 60.

[265] Hey (2002), op. cit. P. 22.

[266] Heath, Chris. "Denby Dale and Upper Denby: Unknown and Unseen." Pen and Sword, 2017. P. 51.

[267] Robinson, Leslie. "Remembering Marshall Mill, Scissett." Denby Dale Parish Council, 2010. P. 3.

[268] Sp. St. 60353/171. P. 195.

[269] Hey et al (2007), op. cit. P. 373.

[270] Redmonds, op. cit. P. 523.

[271] Hinchliffe, David. "Descent into Silence: Cawthorne's Forgotten Tragedy." Scratching Shed Publishing, 2021. P. 68.

[272] Heath (2006), op. cit. P. 26.

[273] Ibid.

[274] See leaflet "Short Walks From High Flatts" in 'Walking in the East Peak' series. Discover East Peak, Kirklees MC and Denby Dale Parish Council.

[275] Sp. St. 60249/64.

[276] Morehouse, op. cit. P. 105.

[277] Ibid. P. 106.

[278] Sp. St. 60236/51.

[279] Sp. St. 60376/194/4.

[280] Dransfield, op. cit. P. 14.

[281] Sp. St. 60321/139.

[282] Turner, op. cit. P. 362.

[283] Surtees Society. "Depositions from the Castle of York relating to Offences Committed in the Northern Counties in the Seventeenth Century", Vol XL. London, 1861. P. 209.

[284] Hoyle, op. cit. P. 404.

[285] Waddell, Brodie, ed. "Petitions in the State Papers, 1600-1699". British History On-Line.

[286] Cross, John. "The Curate and the King's Coin." Shalliley Books, 2019. P. 42.

[287] Ibid. P. 69.

[288] Hey, David. "Yorkshire from AD 1000". Longman, 1986. P. 202.

289 Dransfield, op. cit. P. 18.

290 Heath (2017), op cit. P. 53.

291 Green, op. cit. P. 33.

292 "The Time of Our Lives in Heath." Heath Residents Association, 2000. P.106.

293 Ibid. P. 45.

294 Walker, J. W. "Wakefield: Its History and People." EP Publishing, 1939. Vol 2, P. 623.

295 C/8/412/11. National Archives.

296 Hunter, op. cit. Vol. 2. P. 346.

297 Taylor, Kate (Ed.). 'Newland splendour reduced to rubble' in "Wakefield District Heritage". Pub. Wakefield E.A.H.Y. Committee, 1976. P.12.

298 C/8/412/11. National Archives.

299 Ibid.

300 On-line source.lowercalderlegends.wordpress.com

301 Fletcher, op. cit. P. 179.

302 "Denby 1841 Census Returns". Huddersfield and District Family History Society. P. 20.

303 Pickering, op. cit. P. 22.

304 Sharpe, op. cit. P. 174.

305 Winsham, op. cit. P. 1.

306 Peel, op. cit. P. 180.

307 Bamford, Holly. "Re-examining Community Dynamics in Witchcraft Trials." Lecture at Leeds University on 19 April, 2023, sponsored by the Sheffield Centre for Early Modern Studies.

308 Sharpe, J. A. "Witchcraft in Seventeenth Century Yorkshire: Accusations and Counter Measures." Borthwick Institute, 1992. P. 18.

309 Surtees Society, op. cit. P. 208.

310 Ibid.

311 Hoyle, op. cit. P. 403.

312 Pickering, op. cit. P. 7.

313 Sharpe, (1997), op. cit. P. 216.